RELATIONAL DATABASES:
Concepts, Selection and Implementation

A. J. Page

SIGMA PRESS – Wilmslow, United Kingdom

First published in 1990 by

Sigma Press, 1 South Oak Lane, Wilmslow, Cheshire SK9 6AR, England.

Reprinted 1992

British Library Cataloguing in Publication Data

A CIP catalogue record for this book is available from the British Library.

ISBN: 1-85058-140-1

Typesetting and design by

Sigma Hi-Tech Services Ltd

Printed in Malta by

Interprint Ltd.

Distributed by

John Wiley & Sons Ltd., Baffins Lane, Chichester, West Sussex, England.

Acknowledgement of copyright names

Within this book, various proprietary trade names and names protected by copyright are mentioned for descriptive purposes. Full acknowledgment is hereby made of all such protection.

Preface

I remember vividly, when sitting a board interview with the Civil Service many years ago, being asked to describe a Relational Database Of course at that time I didn't know how to reply to the question, so it is a little ironic that I now come to write this book, which above all seeks to answer just this question. Between that time and now, I have gained extensive experience of three Relational products, namely Ingres, Oracle and perhaps a less known, but equally significant product, the DBC/1012 Database Computer and have often presented or demonstrated these products to potential purchasers. It was in fact these presentations and conversations with people interested in investing in relational technology, that made me decide to write this book. It seemed to me to that, although great amounts of time, effort and care were taken in evaluating different relational products, very rarely was I convinced that the purchasers either knew the complete story or were basing decisions on reality rather than theory.

The book is thus born out of my own experience and focuses on three themes. Firstly on relational concepts including both some history and possible future developments. Secondly it details some of the more important facilities that a Relational Database Management System (RDBMS) should provide and, lastly, real-life examples and viewpoints illustrate the practicalities of using an RDBMS.

There are two major parts. Part 1 seeks to define both what databases are and how they are used. It describes the differences between Relational Databases and their predecessors, and details the relational model by describing its close affinity with data normalisation techniques. Chapter 5 describes the different the various database architectures used to support current products, and in this I rely heavily on my experiences with Oracle, Ingres and the Teradata DBC/1012. I realise that in time my descriptions of these products will become out of date, but this is unavoidable.

A logical step from database architectures takes us into a chapter devoted to On-Line Transaction Processing and to complete Part 1, I have illustrated the 12 rules that were formulated by E. F. Codd to define a Relational Database.

Part 2 is devoted to describing some of the more common and important facilities that should be provided in an (RDBMS). I have used the three aforementioned products to illustrate these facilities, and again I lay myself open to the possibility (indeed certainty), that my descriptions will become out of date. I have not attempted to cover all the facilities that should be on offer, and perhaps the two most noteworthy that I have omitted are the use of Structured Query Language (SQL) from inside Third Generation Languages (embedded SQL), and the close affinity of relational systems with Fourth Generation Languages (4GL). Both of these subjects deserved a greater degree of discussion than I can manage in a book of this nature.

Topics that are covered in Part 2 include a discussion on SQL (Chapter 8) followed by Chapters 9 and 10 covering the topics of indexing and optimisation. Following these performance-oriented chapters, the next two are concerned with transaction management and detail both the concept of a transaction and the required locking mechanisms that can make them work. Next I have included a chapter covering security and follow this with a description of integrity constraints. Journalling, Auditing and Dictionaries are each dealt with in separate chapters. Finally, I have brought the book to a close with a chapter on the subject of the Distributed Relational Database which may be of use to people involved in the evaluation of such architectures.

I have started each chapter with an indicator of its subject matter, and have tried at the end of each, to summarise the major points to be found within the chapter and points that should be considered in more depth when reviewing that particular subject.

Finally, let me say that writing this book was a very educational and enjoyable experience for me. I thank all who helped me and those who simple put up with me during those long hours in front of a PC, and I hope that all who read this book will learn something, no matter how small. I also thank the people in Oracle, Ingres and Teradata who have helped me directly or otherwise, in my understanding of their products – I hope I have done them justice in this book.

Jon Page

Contents

PART 2:
RELATIONAL DATABASE
MANAGEMENT SYSTEMS

Introduction

The world of the programmer today stands at something of a crossroad. Rarely before has there been such a wide variety of specialisms awaiting mastery and never before have the rewards for those that have mastered them been so disproportionately scaled against those that have not. Changes occur every day and the industry has gone through many times of uncertainty. There have been battles between the Mainframe diehards and the micro computer innovators. Mini computers have often been used to avoid decision making and many of our large blue chip industries have changed their strategic hardware and software policies so often that lack of decision making becomes a real productivity problem.

Now however, there are even more choices to be made. In addition to those that previously demanded our attention, we must now consider Relational Database software, Fourth Generation Languages and Expert Systems to name just a few. We must also understand that these items, coupled with hardware, are all likely to be interrelated by some overall company requirement. What is the role of these Relational Databases, Fourth Generation Languages and Expert Systems and is technology at last advancing at a faster rate than we can assimilate? These are all valid issues and in this book I have attempted to supply some of the answers regarding the use of Relational Databases.

From the view point of the DP professional there is little benefit in today's climate of either standing the middle ground or of being the 'jack of all trades'. The third generation of computer languages, and those that swear by them, find themselves in the middle of the road whereas yesterday they not only built the road but also decided in what direction it was to go. In the blink of an eye, instead of three generations of programming language there are now at least five, and the people who invested everything in their third generation expertise, find themselves severely out in the cold. These people must now learn new skills to survive, or perhaps revert to older ones long forgotten.

Not to be outdone by the great progress being made in the development of programming languages, advance in the design of data storage methods has not been slow, and to keep a certain symmetry, I have tried to define five generations of database structure to match the well-documented five generations of programming language. Whilst there is certainly some relationship in the way the languages and databases have grown up, this relationship is not always clear, as you will see.

1

By way of introducing the subject of this book, I would like to pause for a while and examine in broad terms the software evolution that we have witnessed in the last few decades.

It is common, and in fact I already have done so, to refer to the evolution of computer languages in terms of 'generations', the first of which, not surprisingly enough, called the 'first generation'. This refers back to the days when all computer instructions were coded, and often toggled into the machine in binary. It was indeed a very primitive and labour intensive activity, and one certainly prone to many errors. Thankfully, and very quickly, it was discovered to be a lot easier to devise codes for these long-winded binary instructions and to feed these codes to the machine to be assembled into the binary 'machine instructions' required. This represented the jump from first to second generation programming languages.

It was a large and revolutionary step. Instead of pandering to the computer and having to spoon feed it in its own 'yes or no' language, the programmer could write in codes and symbols more understandable to himself and others, and let a software tool, the assembler, convert these instructions into the explicit bit configurations understood by the hardware. As the instructions became easier to write and understand so productivity increased, a factor which benefited further from the fact that single 'assembler language' statements could represent many instructions at the 'machine code' level.

Just as assembler programs could thus become more sophisticated and procedural, a progression in the idea of such programs manipulating data dawned, and although at this stage such data tended to be simple in structure and low in volume, rapid advancement was awaiting round the corner.

Let me take this opportunity of stating that, for the purpose of this introduction, my idea of a database is simply that of a store of data, in any format and of any volume. At the lowest level of programming, databases took the form of simple areas of storage, defined as variables or arrays within programs. The contents of such 'databases' were 'hard coded' into the program, or otherwise created, destroyed or manipulated without reference to any datastore outside the context of that program. As such, data existed as combinations of lists, arrays, variables and literals and even at this stage the limitations of such data storage techniques were easily recognisable; a fact that led quickly to the separation of the data (database) and code (programs) as two separate entities. Indeed, this simple action represented a major advancement in the concept of data storage and management, which took the sophistication of the database itself from its first to its second generation.

It is a recognisable phenomenon within the industry that advancement in design comes with a continued and increasing abstraction from lower levels of detail. Just as assembler languages separated the programmer to a great extent from the physical machine, whilst still within themselves remaining essentially machine specific, the third generation of languages provided tools that went three stages further, to bring dramatic increases in productivity. Firstly, they enable the generation of many assembler level instructions from brief and simple commands, which were themselves designed with much greater thought and consideration to the human interface. Secondly, they sought to implement standard languages that were usable across different types of machine. Thus whilst the assembler programmer must learn largely different assembler languages, if he should switch from IBM to ICL machines, and indeed often between systems manufactured by the same supplier, he would find surprisingly little difference in the dialects of COBOL in use, because all the low level differences are ironed out by the respective COBOL compilers. The third major enhancement saw the inclusion of standard methods, within the languages, to structure and access data stores, which at this stage are more commonly referred to as files. Whilst third generation languages still support the first generation of database, by facilitating the definition and storage of data structures and values entirely within the program, there was however, a rapid movement to hold all data externally in files. These data files then became accessible to many different programs simultaneously. It must be said that in achieving this, languages were extended with both a mishmash of operating-system-specific commands, and those that were destined to become industry standard in the field of file handling.

Very quickly dawned the realisation that the act of storing, structuring and accessing data could be optimised and that many fundamental issues arising from the inherent independence of data, such as security, currency and access control, could be centralised. This led to the creation of the third generation database in the form of the all encompassing Database Management System, supported originally by both specialised software and extension to the current third generation languages.

In fact, the penetration of the Database Management System (DBMS) is now almost complete within data processing environment, and nearly all computer manufacturers supply both file handling capability and DBMSs accessible to all languages supported by their systems. However, in many ways this has represented a step back from true advancement, because the DBMSs that were built, were designed initially to support specific types of application on specific hardware platforms, and so did not truly progress the concept of the independent data repository. It is true also that the methods of accessing these structures ensured that the languages used, once again became machine dependent simply because the DBMSs they referenced were themselves not portable between machines or operating systems. Of course, this problem should be seen in context. If the majority of commercial computers in the world are IBM, the fact that, as an IBM programmer, you know IBM's major third generation database offering, IMS and the methods required to access it, puts you in a very strong position compared to the person that understands well the COBOL extensions required to access the Data General INFOS system. Portability is a worthwhile goal only if combined with profitability, and indeed at the corporate level perceptions change. The company that has locked its data into an IDMS database is going to find it very difficult and expensive to change its computer strategy to incorporate increasingly smaller, distributed machines from a different manufacturer. The potential, however, for such changes, and the financial implications of them, are becoming more significant as every day goes by.

The requirement at this stage for beneficial progress, was for a simplification of the way data was seen to be stored and was available to be accessed; in short, a further level of abstraction from the third generation database and language.

It was a simple realisation that if the entire industry all used the same simple logical way of representing, storing and accessing data, then in one sweep, enormous productivity benefits would arise, as data, code and skills became portable, and the science became more easily understood and accessible to the people it serves.

It's pleasing to note that by and large this realisation has been accepted, and this logical view of data which the new generation of both languages and databases supports, is defined on mathematically proven set theory. The term relational has arrived, and has given opportunities to all and sundry to build new products, or advance older ones, so that they store data logically, in terms of flat, two-dimensional tables or relations. Similarly, a growth industry lies in providing the tools that can manipulate this data through the new database access language SQL, and to provide new human interfaces whose ease of use reflects the enormous strides the new culture had made into simplification. We can therefore see, that the fourth generation of both language and database arose together and as mutual partners.

Probably at this level, we see the clearest and most direct relationship between a generation of languages and its equivalent generation of databases. It is certainly true, and has been a necessity in achieving upgrade paths, that most third generation languages can access fourth generation databases (relational), and likewise many fourth generation languages (4GLs) can access many third generation databases, but in truth there is a very close kinship between the fourth generation products. It is hard to imagine 4GLs being successful without the inherent simplicity of the relational database, and conversely it would seem futile to plough effort into developing more simple database products if this simplicity could not be reflected in the programming tools that support them. There is certainly great room for improvement here yet, and so today there is both a huge presence of 3GL products, and an increased penetration of 4GL products and concepts. So what then for the future and the fifth generation database in particular?

It's probably the case, and will continue to be for some time, that the programmer's life is destined to be spent providing applications specific to very concise and often complicated business problems, and we have sought, or been forced, to put several barriers in between the data and the person that wishes to derive information from it. Typically these barriers have been in the form of hardware, software and people whose task, in simple terms, has been to change data into such information.

The role of the fifth generation, both language and database, should, I believe, seek to cut away this barrier, and allow the end-user to extract information directly from data quickly, with flexibility, and based on volumes unthought of at present.

My view therefore of fifth generation database products may be fulfilled when these databases can make better use of specialised hardware, perhaps in the form of general purpose database machines. I would like to see them lowered in status to that of a simple utility, much perhaps as communications functions have been off-loaded from mainframes. We now commonly accept that many communications functions are executed in dedicated 'front-end' processors, and perhaps database activity should also be 'black boxed' as a 'back-end' processor in its fifth generation. Certainly such databases should interface to many different host computers, and many different software packages, and be served with many different development tools. It must be relational in the logical sense, and be capable, both of holding enormous quantities of data, and of delivering the necessary through-put. It will be fault tolerant, available 24 hours a day, and almost certainly built in such a fashion as to provide linear processing expandability. Perhaps as important as any, will be its ability to exhibit some degree of intelligence in providing support for an improved version of SQL. This 'new SQL' must have much greater awareness itself of data structures, so it can relieve the end user of this particular and tiresome burden. To illustrate this last point let's remember that whilst it is indeed a huge improvement to write, for example, in SQL:

SELECT * FROM SALARIES WHERE NAME = 'Jon'

than write the 50 or so lines needed to do the same in COBOL, when we can say:

GIVE ME Jon's SALARY

and have a quick response, we will possibly have managed the move from fourth generation environments and be preparing for the fifth.

However, we are not quite at this heady level as yet, and although there are products, or rather combinations of products, that can achieve the above to some extent today, through the use of specialised hardware (and indeed one of these, namely Teradata's DBC/1012 database machine, is used to a small degree to illustrate various points made within this book), there is still a long way to go.

Fifth generation products are not my prime concern at this present time however, when I witness how poorly we are coming to terms with the fourth generation, and it is indeed at this level that this book is directed. Although, as I have illustrated, the progression to 4GLs and Relational Database Management Systems is largely a natural one, prompted very much by that of applications backlogs and the need for increased simplicity, it seems to me that there are a great many installations of these products that are not benefiting fully from their presence .

This may be due largely to a lack of clear direction when evaluating, buying, using and supporting the products. I think it is fair to say that the relational model of data as defined by E Codd several years ago now, and explained later in this book, is proving its practical worth, and now is implementable in a variety of software products which have themselves proved their excellence. Indeed when combining the rediscovered concepts of analysis and design, such as Third Normal Form (TNF) and Entity Relationship modelling, with the excellence of some of the current RDBMSs available, and such automated development techniques as Computer Aided Systems Engineering (CASE), DP managers should be revelling in a flurry of software development progress.

However, this scenario is very rarely achieved in the real world, and it seems likely that the reason why this is true, is that the scale and scope of the modern day Relational Database System is not appreciated by purchasers, and is not emphasised by the vendors. This is indeed an unfortunate combination that often ensures that the products under-achieve in terms of their true capabilities. Let us expand this idea and throw some light on current RDBMS usage.

In the recent past, the word database has often conjured up pictures of large installations with large machines, enormous amounts of data, and thousands of on-line terminals. Such a database, more often than not, belongs in my third generation and would typically be built around an IMS or IDMS type product, supported by teams of system programmers and a Database Administration team responsible for the 'corporate data'. The database held data, structured as in the 'corporate data' model, defined by an autonomous design group – the Data Administration. It is a fairly obvious reality that an entity of this size represents a large investment, in many senses of the word, and is of limited flexibility. In the time frame required to build such database applications, the business requirements to be met by them invariably change. Unfortunately, the architecture which the data structures were founded upon were not easily changed, in either physical or logical terms, and certainly the programming tools used to access these structures were complex and procedural. Even worse, the structure of the data was directly reflected in the applications that used that data, and so a picture emerges of a three-fold problem:

❑ huge investment

❑ limited flexibility

❑ poor programming tools giving low productivity

As an aside, and when considering these problems, it is tempting to forget what I believe to be the ultimate fallacy – that of the 'corporate database', but I fear that here is not the time or the place to elaborate on this concept.

The picture illustrated above is still in major evidence now, and the realisation of such problems in some large IBM installations for example, is responsible for a growing move to the strategic relational offering from IBM: DB2. This illustrates indeed, the paradox of the RDBMS. In an IBM world, DB2 will replace (co-existing initially with) IMS and other large DBMSs because it will be seen as their equivalent, or greater, in all areas of functionality including speed. For this reason DB2 installations are likely to be successful, ambitious, beneficial and productive (given of course that the product itself proves to be usable), because its perceived importance as a strategic tool will ensure the presence of staff, and commitment to make it work, both from the user and IBM itself.

In the non-IBM world, it is rare that a RDBMSs will be seen in the same light, and it is common to find them being used as slightly superior file handlers, losing many of the advantages of the products, and thus down-grading their contribution and status to something a good deal less than they deserve. Thus, we have a fairly common scenario: in order to solve some easily perceivable problems – the applications backlog for example – senior management is suffering from muddled thinking, by envisaging an RDBMS as a quick and easy solution to systems building. In fact this is a false idea, and is fundamental to the reason why realised productivity gains are lower than expected in most cases. The answer really, and it does work when managed realistically, is that the products can be used to help clear application backlogs, but to be successful requires not only fourth generation products, but a methodology ensuring their beneficial use, based on a clearly defined relational database strategy. This should be defined in just as much detail, and with just as much commitment, as one might assume from any other more traditional large-scale database implementation.

In order to conclude this introduction therefore, and to throw some further light on the subject, I believe that in the long-term it is almost certain that the relational world will split into two fragments – DB2 and the rest, and that this is not altogether a bad thing. I think it unlikely that products, such as Oracle and Ingres, will establish and maintain a large presence in the IBM world, and in fact history tells me that DB2 will only have to be somewhere "as good as" other products to win enormous market share. Perhaps the main threat to DB2 will be from the specialist database machines, which will almost certainly remain quicker and more capable of handling enormous quantities of data. These are finding their market niche right now.

The non-IBM world is currently looking no further than a handful of products, including the well-known Ingres and Oracle systems, but with fair competition arising from all quarters. All of these products will be offering the same types of facilities, so whilst in this book I have illustrated facilities and architectures, often with reference to Oracle and Ingres, I have made strenuous efforts to avoid bias to any particular product. Indeed I have often illustrated certain facilities, knowing full well that they will be out of date by the time this book is published, but I feel that it is often the background to relational products that is so interesting, and sheds light on their current state.

Table 1 The Evolution of Database and Language

Generation	Language	Database
1	Peeking and Poking Machine code	Arrays, Lists Variables etc
2	Assemblers	Files
3	3GLs – COBOL FORTRAN, BASIC	DBMS – IMS, IDMS, ADABAS FILES – SERIAL, SEQUENTIAL, RANDOM, ISAM
4	4GLs – SQL FORMS ABF, FOCUS, SQL??	Relational DBMS Oracle, Ingres, DB2
5	Non-procedural Intellectual Natural language WIMP interface INTELLECT, AION	Database Machines? BL8000 DBC/1012

Part I

What is a Database?

1

The Use of Databases

Whilst the second part of this book concerns itself with the functionality of Relational Database Management Systems, Part 1 tries to explain the reasons why they are important within the DP industry. Before progressing into the detailed world of the relational product it's perhaps relevant to spend some time putting it into perspective by examining such general topics as what databases actually are and how they are used. These two specific issues are covered in the two opening chapters of this book. This first chapter sets out to examine some possible strategies for using database technology. It does not wish to instruct on how databases should best be used, but seeks instead to draw attention to the fact that a database strategy, if not implemented with plain thinking and commitment, is unlikely to succeed.

The advantages of relational techniques and products over any predecessors are without question, but without the qualities mentioned above, mediated with a great amount of pragmatism, failure awaits with open arms. It is not enough just to use Relational Databases, you must understand why you are using them, and what you hope to achieve by doing so.

The Role of the Database

In the present marketplace, it is possible to implement relational products in a variety of ways, at a variety of different costs, and with an associated wide degree of commitment. To set the scene for the rest of this book it is worth exploring the role of the database, and particularly its relational implementation, with the aim of clarifying its position and justifying its popularity.

For an investment of just a few hundred pounds, one can install an off-the-shelf application running under an RDBMS on a PC, with no commitment at all to the RDBMS or its ideology. It's also possible that the same application could be run on a much larger machine, with a proportionately larger community of users, again with little commitment to the actual RDBMS or knowledge of it. This book is aimed at people who are looking to invest, or have invested, in a future commitment to building a relational environment for the development of their own application systems. Such an environment could be equally pertinent to an installation of just a few people and small amounts of hardware, as to a large network of different types of machine, each needing to access shared data pools, with minimum delay and maximum flexibility. Most of the issues are the same, although the strategies adopted may not be.

Levels of Database Implementation

It is true that different strategies of data storage are appropriate to different types of usage, and not all data organisations can hope to provide optimum facilities across the board. In the Relational/4GL world it is wise to have a clear idea as early as possible of the approach that is to be taken, and the results expected, when organising database usage. The wise will have thought a strategy through to some conclusion, before selecting and implementing the product or products required to support it. In order to qualify some of these strategies, let me begin by dividing data environments into five levels of usage.

Level 1 Environment

At this level no DBMS is installed, and instead, data is held in sets of unrelated files. In general, data is not shared between applications in any true sense, and data structures (files) are designed and populated as required by the defined functionality of specific applications. In time, a large proliferation of files grows up, with high redundancy, leading to high maintenance costs. Seemingly trivial changes to applications trigger chain reactions of other changes, and hence become slow and expensive. Change is thus resisted.

Level 2 Environment

A DBMS is used but there is no sharing of data between applications. Separate databases are created for separate applications. This level of implementation is relatively easy to attain, but results in a large proliferation of databases, with the resultant high degree of data redundancy, similar to the file environment of level 1. This scenario can become expensive, and does not realise the major advantages of database operation.

Level 3 Environment

Application independent databases are created, the data content being designed and stored largely independently of the functions to which it will be put, but dependent instead on the relationships existing between data items. Data for business subjects such as customers, products or invoices are associated in shared databases which will later be termed 'enterprise oriented'. At this level, considerable commitment will be needed to ensure sound database designs, but it should ultimately lead to quicker application development, and to lower maintenance costs. This approach requires a change in design and analysis methods from more traditional approaches, and needs skillful management to avoid disintegration to level 2.

Level 4 Environment

This level usually includes systems used primarily for management information, and tends to be driven by changing and demanding user requirements. These structures tend to hold large quantities of data, and require organisation for fast search and retrieval. They require good end-user query facilities, and lend themselves to the implementation of specialised software or hardware.

Level 5 Environment

This level is increasingly becoming a topic of conversation under the banner of the 'information warehouse'. In essence it reflects a single structure which manages all the data of a company or concern, modelled in a manner reflecting the businesses of that enterprise. It hinges on a top-down analysis of a company's total data availability (maybe 'requirement' is really more pertinent), and a bottom-up analysis of how it needs to be accessed. It is an interesting concept, but its usefulness has not yet been demonstrated, and the practical implementation of it will likely be prohibitive in terms of finance, complexity and man power.

So what is the use of these definitions?

What I have tried to achieve by illustrating these levels, is that although this book is primarily a description of an RDBMS, in terms of the facilities and utilities that should be provided within such a facility. A main concern is also to bring to the forefront the fact that the implementation of a successful relational environment will likely follow the answering of at least three questions in the order given below:

1) Do we wish to go the Database route?

2) Should it be Relational?

3) Which specific product is best for the job?

Let us presume a positive answer to the first question necesssitates, as I hope is projected by this text, a 'yes' answer to question two in turn. However, I do think it is important to understand just why this is so, because experience shows that most effort and time is spent deciding the outcome of question three. This neatly ignores the fundamental issue, which is to be sure in our minds, of the reasons why databases, and more precisely relational databases, can be of benefit. Equally as important of course, is how they should be best utilised to maximise this benefit.

The Utilisation of Databases

Let us continue by sharing some of the different ways in which database technology can be utilised.

By answering 'yes' to the question posed earlier "do we wish to go the database route?" we have explicitly stated that we do not wish to implement a level 1 environment. It is invariably the case that in part, at least, the justification for implementing database strategies will be to replace a currently existing environment of this type. It is almost always the case as well, that even if the immediate target is for application development supported by level 2 or level 3 environments, there will be a call to provide 'management information' at some stage thus necessitating a level 4 set-up sooner or later. It's best to plan for it 'sooner'! Meanwhile someone in authority will need to address the issue of level 2 versus level 3. This really is a tough decision, and if not explicitly chosen and enforced, will invariably default to that of level 2.

Whilst I certainly do not wish to be drawn into detailed debate on the usefulness of the different approaches, it is relevant to point out some practical experience and insights gained from them.

1) A true level 2 environment is difficult to manage effectively, easy to evolve and rather defeats the concept of the database – in the long term it must be avoided. It does however enable the provision of quick results that can be of tremendous benefit to a company embarking on a relational program and seeking to get a 'foot in the door' so to speak.

2) I know of no realistic and effective example of a level 3 environment implemented by Relational DBMSs on a large scale at present.

3) Level 4 environments are notoriously difficult to implement successfully because of the very heavy resource utilisation that they need. It is possible that specialised hardware may be needed to satisfy large data volumes and ad-hoc query requirements.

4) There is a commonly held attitude that it is reasonable to start with sights set on a level 2 environment because it will be a simple matter to migrate later to the more desirable level 3. This is a fallacy and in practice never happens.

5) Level 2 and 3 environments can only rarely be integrated with 4 or 5 in the same database, or even on the same computer, which is a great shame because this is exactly where they should be!

6) Level 5 environments have yet, even conceptually, to prove themselves as a useful goal. Business modelling from the apex of a company downwards is fraught with difficulty because decisions taken at this level are often based on market forces, innovation, tradition, ignorance or sheer brilliance.

7) There is a middle way which can lead to effective utilisation of relational ideas, be productive and provide firm platforms for future technical management or innovation. This middle way should be a strategy based on the following principles:

❏ There is top management support of a corporate database strategy (*not* a corporate database) with a determination to make databases valuable corporate resources.

❏ There is concentration on well-specified profitable uses of databases.

❏ A technically competent data administrator is appointed, who is tightly in control of logical and physical database design. This authority should oversee the design of subject oriented databases (e.g. Customer, Products) so that they can be shared by many applications.

❏ There should be a step-by-step build-up of applications based on the subject databases, each step being small and simple. Many such small projects may run in parallel.

Of course there is no detail in this list. I believe that techniques, such as structured methodologies, TNF and the use of tools such as dictionaries, CASE and IPSES should be part of an overall strategy but prefer not to delve too deeply. The appointment of a skilled DBA should ensure the required incorporation of such technologies.

It should now be clear why I have stressed so much the importance of evaluating carefully the aims and objectives of a relational database implementation. It has been proven time and time again, that without commitment and central control, success will be limited, and I think it is no longer reasonable to blame the vendors of the RDBMS products for such failure. If managed correctly, and selected for relevant projects, they will do the job they were intended to do. Data is an extremely valuable corporate resource affecting productivity, profitability and strategic decisions, and any commodity of such importance requires planning from top management. Such planning should be both business oriented and driven. Technical groups in charge of planning corporate information resources generally fail because of their inability to share the perspective of business requirement, or to understand the overall corporate information need. It is also true that some of the best laid plans of database designers have crashed on the rocks of corporate politics.

Database plans often create political problems, which may be severe, and various factions will oppose them. Often these problems can only be solved when top management makes it clear that it believes that database is the way to proceed, and has signed off on a corporate information systems plan. Remember that the sharing of data in a database, often removes people's feelings of ownership which has both its good and bad points.

So this first chapter can be seen, in some respects, as the posting of a warning. The main content and thrust of the remaining chapters is both an explanation of the history and relevance of the Relational Databases, and a technical dictionary of the current ways in which they are implemented, and of the facilities they offer. The field is exciting, productive and profitable when approached in a reasonable fashion, but it is not a short cut to success. It is usually much more pleasant to drive a four-door saloon than a two-door hatchback, but if you have no need to travel in the first place, then what does it matter? It is also true to say that whichever of the two modes of transport chosen, it is obligatory to have passed your driving test, and very unwise to travel without planning your route or without filling up with petrol and carrying a spare tyre.

It is quite fun to carry on with this analogy, and it is perhaps correct that in a world of Ferraris and Rolls Royces, we leave the Relational Database as the four-door saloon. We may perhaps, choose to see its third generation cousins as more like the Greyhound bus – larger, more expensive, very predictable, but reassuringly reliable.

Summary

1) The DP world has suddenly taken to Relational Databases in a way unprecedented in the past. Often, motives must be questioned, as should some of the methodologies utilised to incorporate these products into overall data strategies.

2) When making the move to relational, do it carefully and with great planning. The first few months will be critical and will pave the way to a successful, or disappointing, future.

3) Having the right attitude to the products available is often more beneficial when selecting which seems to be the best one. All of the more well-known products can either perform well or poorly depending entirely on how they are used and what people's aspirations or expectations are.

2

What is a Database?

A reasonable place to start a book of this nature is to describe what we mean by the term Database before next progressing to expand on the role of a Database Management System. 'Database' is indeed a strange term that is interpreted by many people in various ways, and I've already given one fairly nebulous definition in the Introduction. This chapter expands on this simple idea to set the scene for the rest of this book.

File Management

All suppliers of commercially viable hardware provide within their operating systems some method of handling files. At the lowest level, this will include support for straight serial or sequential files, but equally likely, there will be other more sophisticated structural file types supported, allowing either direct access or some type of indexed retrieval of data. Often a layer of software may be introduced to coordinate an indexed approach, to thus provide a still greater level of sophistication, and it is then a logical progression to allow the full facilities of a DBMS on top of such structures, to provide some level of data recovery, security, optimised access and data consistency. Typically, you may find all options available on a single machine. The Data General Advanced Operating System, for example, supports different primitive file types, sophisticated and navigational indexed access in INFOS II, and a full blown CODASYL DBMS aptly called DBMS. On top of even this there is a relational capability in the form of DG/SQL, and Data General provided tools that access information across all types of their native file managers.

I must stress here that I am certainly not running a sales campaign for Data General, because, in this day and age, this is precisely the environment that we might wish to avoid, as I have previously explained. Anyway it is far from unique, because nearly all manufacturers provide the same scope for file management, or perhaps mismanagement (compare the DEC product range for example).

The Database Management System

Firstly let us try and put the scope of a Database Management System (DBMS) into perspective. In simple terms a DBMS is a mechanism for coordinating the storage and retrieval of data in a manner ensuring its constant integrity, consistency and availability. Thus, if we consider a public library (an example that I shall use again later) and compare it with a sophisticated DBMS, we might consider the contents of the books as being the data stored in a computerised system. In such an analogy the DBMS will reflect the functionality we are so familiar within a library in terms of:

1) Indexes within books, on shelves and on rows within shelves.

2) Card indexes or microfiche used to find books by author or content.

3) The librarian, and all the tasks he or she performs.

4) The list of all library members and which books they currently have out on loan.

5) The mechanisms by which old or damaged books are replaced and new books supplied.

It is fairly clear that if we ripped out the individual pages of each book, and placed them all in a heap in the marketplace of a town and called that the library, it would be of little use to anyone. In fact, the full library function would be lost if any of the above layers of management, or others that I have not included, were not in place and understood to be in place. Whilst I am not saying that it is common to find computer held data in a form quite as bad as pictured above, it is common to see that whilst the pages remain in the books, the books themselves are strewn randomly across the marketplace. In the precise industry that we refer to in this book, this is far from ideal, so what then contributes to making a Database Management System successful?

Many books have been devoted to this specific question, so I wish to be very brief in my dealings with it because really, a DBMS is all things to all men, depending just where you are viewing it from.

Basically all items of data have at least four important attributes and these are:

❏ a name by which the data is known

❏ a physical description

❏ a value

❏ relationships with other data

Put quite simply, it is the job of the DBMS to record these four characteristics of every item of data defined to it, and to store this data in a manner whereby:

1) Access to it is controlled.

2) Its consistency, currency and integrity are always ensured.

3) Physical resource utilisation is optimised

4) Information about the data stored (often termed 'metadata') is available.

Of course these four factors themselves are often extremely complex and interrelated, covering such topics as locking, restart/recovery, before and after image journalling, indexes, clusters and dictionaries. I have made stringent efforts in the second part of this book to define and explain most of the important facilities that go together to establish a DBMS, which, in reality, should be seen as a family of tools, utilities and control features which manage the total data resource. I am therefore not going to define the DBMS here, but it is useful to explain just why the 'database' part of a DBMS differs from a random set of files and the previous rather low-level definition given in the Preface.

To Begin at the Beginning

A prerequisite of building a useful database is to understand why we are building it, what data we hope to store in it, how the data is related, and also how we intend to access it (this last factor is debatable and need not always be true as we will see later). This knowledge is derived from adequate problem and data analysis, coupled with structured vetting techniques, such as Third Normal Form analysis, to name just one.

Commonly a result of such analysis is expressed in terms of Entities, Attributes and the Relationships that exist between them, and these are brought together in a Logical Data Model of the enterprise under analysis. Whilst talking terms, this paper model is often called an ERA or Entity, Relationship, Attribute model.

It's worth explaining some of these terms at this stage. Entities are the objects of concern in the enterprise we are trying to model (Customers and Products in a sales order system, for example) and Attributes are all the factors we use, or can use, to describe such entities (Customer Address and Product Description perhaps). Entities tend to have either indirect or direct relationships with each other, and these are modelled as well. These may take the form of a specific Product being held in stock by a specific Supplier (a direct relationship) or a Customer being related to a Product, perhaps by a Sales Order – an indirect relationship.

This book is not concerned with analysis techniques, so I will leave any further explanation, presuming anyone reading this will be sufficiently familiar with this form of analysis 'jargon'.

The point of the above is that a database, in my refined view, is not simply a set of random data that 'exists' and is to be used, but rather is a collection of related and structured data. In reality, this group of data will have been defined to solve specific applications problems, and not to specify the requirements of a business per se. For this reason I am not encouraging the concept of the Corporate Database in this book. The purpose of the DBMS is to project a logical view of a modelled enterprise, onto a physical, computer-based bed of software and hardware in such a way that we as users can manipulate occurrences of entities, attributes and relationships. Such manipulation should be attainable with whatever software tools or applications we choose, and performed at the logical level leaving the DBMS (as our physical interface to the data) to translate our logical requests to whatever is required physically to maintain our model, or retrieve our data. The DBMS must action such requests, whilst providing some degree of protection from being asked to do unacceptable, or unauthorised activities. Thus a fundamental role of the DBMS is to preserve both a logical and a physical occurrence of the data supporting one (or more than one) particular enterprise. In fact there is a further layer to concern ourselves with as well as we shall now see.

The Three-layered Database

We can describe a DBMS conceptually, physically and in terms of software functionality, not as a two- but as a three-layered animal. This holds true for all different types of DBMS to some extent, and is especially pertinent to the relational world as we shall see later. The three layers can be shown diagrammatically as follows:

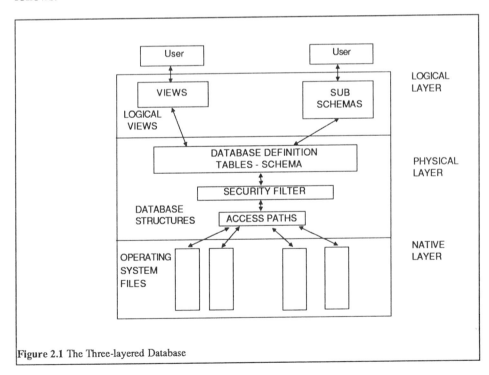

Figure 2.1 The Three-layered Database

Whilst I shall explain these levels shortly, I must add that this view is certainly not original, although the terms external, conceptual and internal are in more widespread circulation than my own: logical, physical and native.

By way of explanation, I have introduced my own terms in preference at this stage, simply because I believe that they more closely represent the different ideas implemented at the different layers. I justify them largely because they are more easy to understand and remember. At the 'native' layer for example, the DBMS software is talking directly to a specific operating system – that which is 'native' to the machine. Physical best associates the 'middle level' with what a Database Administration (DBA) or project member will know as Physical Database Design, an activity which is explicitly defining the database at the level of files, indexes, authorisations etc. The logical level allows implementation of the 'user view' of the data, which will more closely match the preferred data model of the enterprise, and overcomes some of the physical compromises that were made at the physical level.

To summarise this model, the DBMS should allow individual views of the database in very precise, secure and logically correct terms. These views should be defined by a person in some authority – usually the DBA – from a pool of physical data available throughout the database itself. In turn, whilst the DBA protects the end-user from complexity inherent at the physical layer, by only letting him peer through the logical one, the DBMS itself seeks to protect the DBA from the low-level mappings of his physical data structures onto the machine itself.

So we can think of it this way: The logical layer reflects what the user wants to see whilst the physical layer is the mapping of this to the actual structures supported by the chosen RDBMS. The native layer is the mapping of the structures, defined at the physical layer, to structures supported by the underlying operating system.

At this stage let us look at these levels more closely.

The Logical or External Layer

The user interface is positioned at the logical layer, be it either interactive or batch. The user will usually have access only to a strictly controlled subset of the total data held in the database, either through an application or direct query. At this level all thoughts of security, access paths, performance and data storage mechanisms should not be required from the user, and the view of the database should reflect the logical data model as perceived by him.

The Physical or Conceptual Layer

At the physical layer, the native and logical layers are made known to each other as a set of conceptual data structures. These define both the data held at the native layer and relate that data to the users in a logical form that they will understand. The physical layer will thus be a conglomeration of all the physical structures necessary to provide optimised user access and security, and of course at this level, all structures that support the logical data structure must be defined, (relational VIEWS for example).

The Native or Internal Layer

At the native layer, data held within the database is stored in whatever file handling system is appropriate to the target operating system. The storage structures at this level, be they VMS RMS files or IBM VSAM for example, should be absolutely transparent to applications or users of that data. In fact, even the DBA of the database should only be involved at this level when insuring correct access permissions to the base data structures, and maybe to ensure their correct device location etc. Note that if the database is distributed, then the native layer may encompass more than one machine, and even more than one type of operating system.

Now, if we can start thinking about DBMSs as being fundamentally three-layered, all sorts of things become clear. Take a look, for example, at how people, or more correctly functions, interact with the database.

Table 2.1 The Relationship Between Function and Layer	
LEVEL	*PEOPLE*
Logical layer	Database Administration
	Users
	Applications
	Tools
Physical layer	Database Administration
	Operations
	Prototyping programmers
Native layer	Systems programmers
	Operations

At the different levels there are also different languages in use as listed in Table 2.2 on the opposite page.

Indeed the concept of a three-layered database is of great importance, and shows us several things that form the heart of a database system. Because of their importance, it is worth listing them here as a form of summary:

❏ A DBMS allows a clear conceptual break between logical database design and physical database design. As this distinction becomes greater, we can implement applications in a much more logical and flexible manner.

❏ Many logical views of the database can be supported by one physical implementation of it.

Table 2.2 The Relationship Between Language and Layer

LEVEL	LANGUAGE
Logical layer	Fourth Generation Languages
	Query tools
	Sub-schema definition languages
	Data Manipulation Languages
	SQL
Physical layer	Data Definition languages (DDL)
	Schema definition languages
	SQL
Native layer	Operating system command language

❏ Different tools, and even different people interact with the DBMS at different levels.

Whilst a great deal of importance, quite rightly, lies with the distinction between the logical and physical layers, some vendors have achieved significant commercial advantage by leveraging the clear separation of the physical from the native. This separation can either provide immense portability of the RDBMS between machines or tremendous optimisation to specific hardware. In short, the crux of the matter is flexibility, and whilst this goal is not always achieved, it is there in the very heart of the database concept and has driven both the creation of the first DBMSs and their evolution through hierarchical, network, inverted list structures to the current relational database.

Summary

1) The word database varies in definition greatly, depending on who you are talking to, and what their involvement with one is. The definition of a Data Base Management System should not alter. It is a functional piece of software with clearly defined roles and responsibilities.

2) The underlying function of a DBMS is to record names, descriptions, values and relationships, and to allow access to this information in a controlled manner, ensuring always that it remains consistent and sensible.

3) Databases should reflect a fundamental architecture of three interacting, but logically separate, layers. The clearer the separation between these layers is then the easier it will be to understand and utilise.

References

C.J. Date, An Introduction to Database Systems Volume II *Addison-Wesley*, (1983)

C.J. Date, A Guide to Ingres *Addison-Wesley*, (1987)

3

Some DBMS History

In the previous chapters I have tried to explain what the database is and some conceptual ways in which it is used and structured. To carry on with this theme, I now wish to explain some history in order to ensure that the reader is aware that Relational Databases did not arise spontaneously but rather evolved from ideas based on far ranging experience. It's no longer true that everyone involved with Relational DBMSs will have progressed through more traditional forms, and this adds relevance, I hope, to this chapter which has proved the most difficult of all to write.

Database Models

The Relational Database, and in fact the whole concept of relational data modelling, has only been with us since the 1980s and is still a very new science to most of us. Database Management Systems, however, go back a good deal longer, and some of the products in common use 20 or so years ago are still in service today and performing comparatively well. Such older products have been conceptually divided into three main groups according to their underlying architectures, namely the hierarchical, network and inverted list structure. It is probably a little unfair to call this chapter by a title that perhaps leads one to believe that its contents refer to some long-ago defunct products, because this is not the case. However, it is true to say that the hierarchical and network database models, which this chapter describes are, to say the least, not 'in vogue' at the present time. Whilst they do account for by far and away the largest investment in database technology at this time, there is certainly a rapid movement away from these types of products. Indeed a fair amount of effort has been expended in trying to make such non-relational systems appear to be relational, at least to the user, and it's interesting to note that the products based on the inverted list scheme have fared comparatively well in this deception. In reality though, the inverted list is not really a database architecture but simply an access method and so it is not described in this text. Products based on it, such as Adabas, are still largely in the fore-front as commercial databases, however, and will command a large market share for some time yet.

The Hierarchical Model

To maintain some chronological accuracy, I must firstly describe the hierarchical form of Database Management System which originated from a specific requirement to model a bill of parts type application in the aviation industry. A 'bill of parts', for those not conversant with such terms, is a structure that is based on the principle of an item being made up of several parts, each of which may also be made up of several others. Attempts were made to mirror such a logical structure in the physical design of a DBMS and the resulting 'hierarchical DBMS' was a software solution that was immediately appealing to the people responsible for the complex data management tasks involved in such sophisticated manufacturing operations. The model that was created was tremendously successful, due in no small part to the fact that the logical structure of the DBMS was not only reflective of the applications problem it was designed to solve, but was also intimately related to the physical way in which it was designed and built. Such a close tie between logical and physical, whilst having the disadvantage of being restricted by the need to predefine all inter-data relationships, can provide excellent performance and indeed this has been the biggest selling point for this type of database.

Due to the success of the model, it was adapted to solve many types of commercial problems where data could be defined in terms of hierarchical structures. However, in time, severe weaknesses became apparent with this type of structure, and few of the benefits that are now perceived as critical to DBMS selection (ease of use, flexibility etc) were ever attainable with it, which is surprising considering its huge popularity.

To understand the strategy behind the hierarchical DBMS, let us first see an example of a hierarchical data tree which may be thought of as a fundamental building block for this type of database.

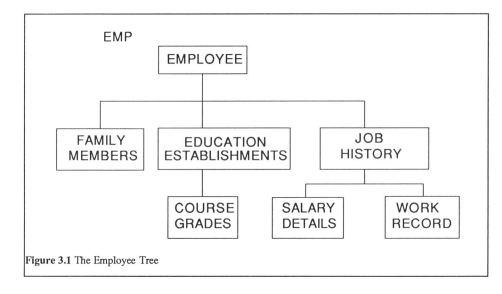

Figure 3.1 The Employee Tree

Let's give this tree the name of EMP, and consider that it represents a logical model of a hierarchical database which is used to record data about Employees. In such a database structure, we can hold several items of data about specific employees, such as their education, including details of courses taken and grades attained, job history in terms of tasks completed, salary earned and family details. The structure will allow us to record, for example, that a specific employee has held several jobs during his career and at each job has progressed through several levels of salary grade, and performed several different tasks within each job. Of course, as is quite usual in this science, the structure is upside-down because the top level of this 'tree' is known as the *root,* and ever increasing detail is revealed as one descends levels. It is also important to bear in mind one further thing – the lines I have drawn in, which basically represent the relationships between the types of data items, are maintained by a system of pointers. Thus in logical terms, every record sits in a slot from which it cannot move because the record 'behind' it, as it were, has a pointer to it and it itself holds a pointer to the next record. Now let us imagine a further tree holding information about jobs. This might be logically represented thus:

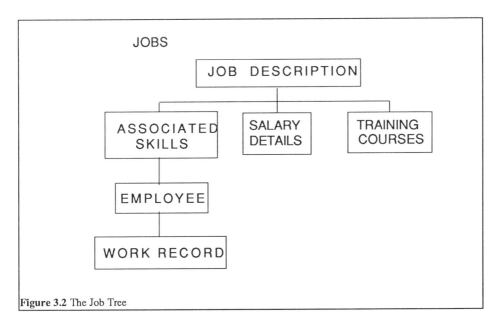

Figure 3.2 The Job Tree

This tree has been named JOB and might be used to record job-related information such as the training requirements required to accomplish a specific task, the salary scales it can command, the skills it needs and the employees who have provided these specific skills in performing this job.

We can see that, if we implemented the two trees so far described as different database structures, we have at least two problems. Firstly the employee work record detail is repeated, so that we have introduced redundant data, and secondly there is no link between the two trees.

In terms of management, this means that if a specific employee gains significant experience of a job, both the EMP and JOB databases need to be updated identically and simultaneously. Furthermore, if one wished to find out which employees had an education that would suit them for particular jobs, then both sets of data would have to be accessed independently and matched in an applications program.

To ease this burden, a hierarchical database is in fact constructed as a set of such trees, each linked to the other at strategic nodes by pointer records, or pointer segments. We might accomplish this in our example by a link across the Employee data to give the following final structure:

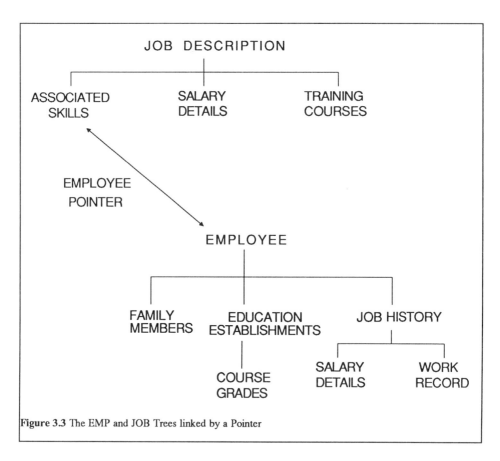

Figure 3.3 The EMP and JOB Trees linked by a Pointer

Thus trees are linked to form bigger trees and any combination of such linked trees can form a database. In this case the EMPLOYEE segment in the EMP tree becomes what is known as a child of the ASSOCIATED SKILLS segment in the JOBS tree and the two are linked by a 'logical child pointer'. We can think therefore, in terms of any tree being made up of one or many other trees, and conversely such trees can usually be broken up into any number of smaller, 'logical' trees. It is these logical 'views' on trees that are accessed and manipulated by applications programs. Taking this idea further, the EMP physical structure can be projected to a specific application maybe only in terms of the following structure, which thus constitutes the applications view of EMP and is termed a logical database or sub-schema.

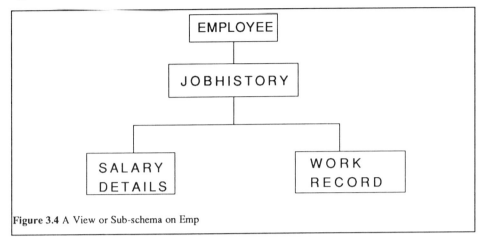

Figure 3.4 A View or Sub-schema on Emp

To summarise so far: this type of database consists of sets of related data hierarchies, each of which can be both logically and physically independent of the others. In reality, these discreet hierarchies are related to each other by key items of data that are linked by physical pointers. These physical pointers are responsible for defining and maintaining inter-data relationships. Different 'views' of either single or multiple hierarchies can be projected, via applications, to the end-user, and these views are defined centrally by the DBA, as sub-schemas.

How then is this data in the database made available to an application? Firstly the complete database will be defined, perhaps by the DBA, as a collection of a number of distinct hierarchical trees as we have already seen. Pointers (relationships) will be defined to link these trees together, thus creating the database as a single definition usually called the Schema. Users will be allowed access to data through specific views or windows onto the database, and these are defined by sub-schemas and represent logical parts of the whole database structure.

In terms of access via an application, the required view or sub-schema is mapped into the application as a buffer area into which records are read from the database, to be manipulated by the application. In the above example, a buffer area in a COBOL application might be defined with field names of EMP,JOB,SAL,EXP for example. Data stored in the database structure is then made available to the application by searching the database in a predefined order, in which the root data is retrieved, followed by presentation of sub-tree data, from left to right, to the applications buffer area. This continues, always processing left to right, until the required records have been accessed and processed.

The fact that this small logical database is part of a much larger related set of data is of no consequence to this particular application which, as I hope to have made clear, is only capable of seeing the items defined in the sub-schema it is using. To illustrate this in our example, let us see the sequence in which data is logically retrieved from such a structure by an application.

Let's take the following data structured as a hierarchy:

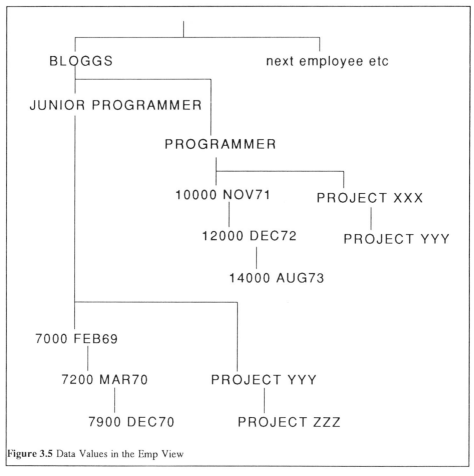

Figure 3.5 Data Values in the Emp View

The order of retrieval of data from the above structure is illustrated on the opposite page.

We should take note therefore, that individual applications do not control or define database structures. These are instead created centrally using specialised languages – the same languages that are also used to make available certain structures to certain applications. Thus one application may see only certain types of records whilst another applications using even the same logical database may be 'sensitive' to a different set.

This is a feature of databases which is of central importance, and worth stressing again here. The subsets of data that an application can see, defined by the DBA, and made available to an application by their mapping in a special file description area,

```
BLOGGS
    ┌ JUNIOR PROG
    │         7000 FEB69
    │         7200 MAR70
    │         7900 DEC70
    │                 PROJECT YYY
    │                 PROJECT ZZZ
    │
    └ PROGRAMMER
              10000 NOV71
              12000 DEC72
              14000 AUG73
                      PROJECT XXX
                      PROJECT YYY

    next employee etc
```

Figure 3.6 Order in which Data is Retrieved from EMP

coded in each application as already mentioned. This area has many names – a program specification block in IBM's DL/1 for example.

Hence in a traditional hierarchical database, we can see three descriptions of data at different levels. At the base level the physical database is defined in terms of segments, fields, lengths, frequency of occurrence, relationships and pointers, access methods and organisation. At a level of abstraction above this sits a definition of the database much as we have described already: entities, attributes and such things as parent/child relationships. This is known generally as the 'schema', there being one schema per database.

Finally and at a layer above this, we find one-to-many discreet 'sub-schemas', each derived from the single schema and each reflecting different logical 'views' on the database which are accessible to users. Such sub-schemas define which data is available to which user, and also in what context in terms of read/write activity, and it is an applications sub-schema that is mapped into the application in order to provide local names to database defined data, as alluded to above.

We will see later how, and the extent to which, this layered approach matches with the relational model and reflects the fundamental layered database approach already described. It should be apparent already though, that the clean cutoff between physical and native layers, that would enable this database structure to become machine independent, is certainly not well-achieved, and is likely impossible with any pointer-oriented system. At this stage, let us just finish discussions on the hierarchical model by considering how it might implement a many-to-many relationship. Suppose we have SUPPLIERs who supply PARTs and whilst a Supplier can supply many types of Parts, a specific Part can also be supplied by many Suppliers. Let us represent this diagrammatically:

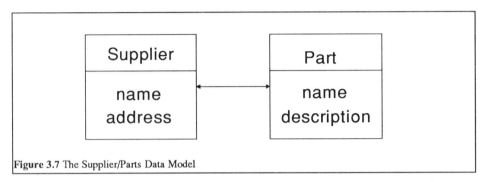

Figure 3.7 The Supplier/Parts Data Model

Now this is a very simple data model indeed, and without a further piece of information, namely *quantity,* its usefulness is questionable. I think in the real world one might wish to know in what quantity a Supplier can provide a specific Part, and if this simple idea, now incorporating the attribute of *quantity,* was modelled as two trees we might have the following structure:

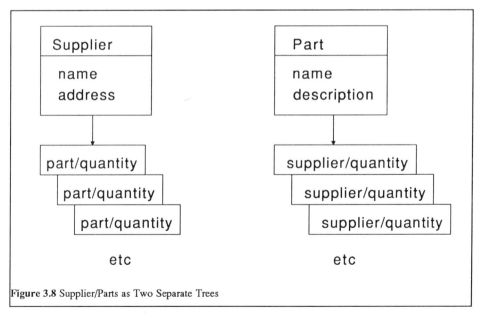

Figure 3.8 Supplier/Parts as Two Separate Trees

Here however, we have implemented redundant data, and caused ourselves a major maintenance problem because if a single Quantity changes, it must be updated in both structures simultaneously with assurances that both values, or none, are successfully updated. We will also have caused ourselves a problem should we wish to create a report with the following data:

Supplier
Name
Address
Part
Quantity
Description

Such a report requires data from both our data trees which would require an application program to perform independent retrievals from both structures and match them internally. In fact such a relationship is implemented in a hierarchical system by way of the aforementioned strategy of logical child pointers.

The data below serves as an example:

Supplier	A	supplies 100 of part 1
Supplier	A	supplies 200 of part 2
Supplier	A	supplies 300 of part 3
Supplier	B	supplies 100 of part 1
Supplier	B	supplies 450 of part 2

If we show such data diagrammatically, we can illustrate the way in which pointers are used to relate items of data, as shown in Figure 3.9 below:

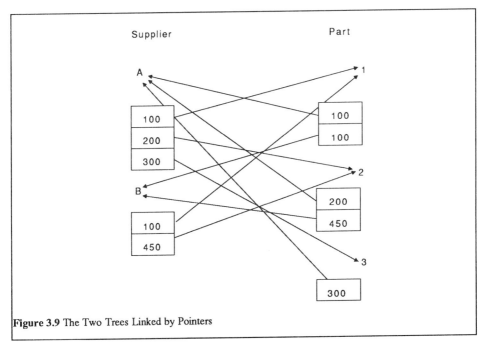

Figure 3.9 The Two Trees Linked by Pointers

We can see from our description so far, that, whilst there is to some extent some conformation to the preferred three-layer approach in the hierarchical structure, the issue is nowhere near as clean as it could be.

The differences between the physical database, and its logical projection to the user or programmer, leave little flexibility, and at the lower levels, the physical and native layers intermingle. This is because at the physical level, all relationships must be defined, in addition to the data storage structures. Even worse, these relationships are maintained by sets of pointers and other mechanisms, which are thus forced into the limelight where we are really seeking to bury them neatly out of sight.

The Network Approach

Following on the heels of the hierarchical database, and as an attempt to improve it, came the Network architecture, now more commonly called the CODASYL database because of the work of this group in defining a standard for it. Again, like the former structure, enormous amounts of design and research have gone into this model, and there are many implementations of it in common use, with the IDMS product probably the front runner. However, the tremendous commercial success of this case only makes one wonder at the eventual penetration of the theoretically enormous improvements within reach in the relational world.

The most noticeable concept of the network model is the replacement of hierarchical tree structures with two level set structures (do not confuse the use of 'set' here with the mathematical entity of the set used when describing the relational model). The set is a new concept, but very simple in essence, being little more than a named two-level relationship as shown below.

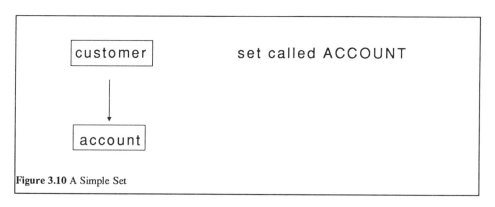

Figure 3.10 A Simple Set

Thus a set called ACCOUNT consists of Customer records (owner) which can each have many Account records (members). Sets can have more than one type of member record, but each such type can only have one owner, so the structure shown in Figure 3.11 on the opposite page is quite valid.

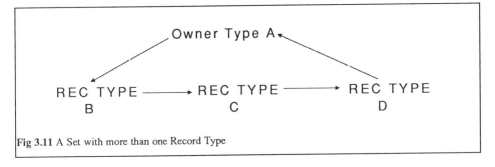

Fig 3.11 A Set with more than one Record Type

Similarly sets can overlap, but must remain only two-level and it is this way that three-level tree-structures can be defined:

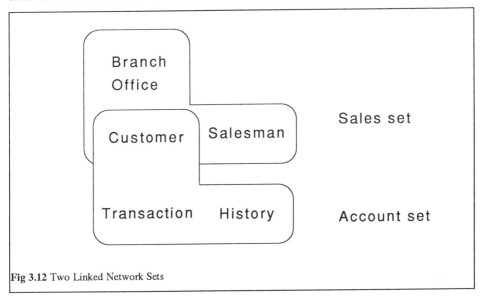

Fig 3.12 Two Linked Network Sets

Thus the familiar hierarchy of tree-type structures is build from sets, where an N-level tree requires at least the presence of N-1 sets and, as the set in effect defines a relationship, it is quite possible to define the same record types in different sets to represent different types of relationship, as illustrated in Figure 3.13 below. Here we have a set of Supplier/Parts records which represent late orders, and by relating these entities by a different set of pointers, we can maintain a set of outstanding orders.

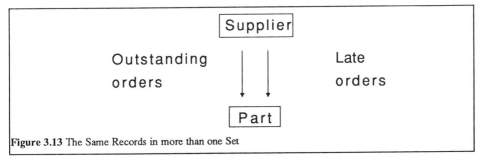

Figure 3.13 The Same Records in more than one Set

Let's look at this in a very simplistic manner: suppose Supplier A has delivered orders for Parts A, G and M and has outstanding orders for X, F and R. The relationships in Figure 3.14 below, which define which set each part belongs in, are actually defined by pointers. So we have:

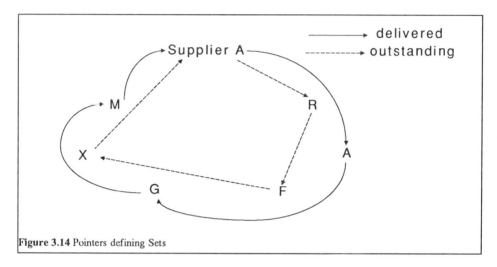

Figure 3.14 Pointers defining Sets

Before progressing further let me utter some words of comfort. Do not worry if by the end of this chapter you don't fully understand the differences between the hierarchical and network approaches. They are fundamentally very similar, one having grown from the other, and it's not always easy to tell them apart.

Let's now revisit our Supplier/Part relationship to show how a many-to-many relationship can be supported in a network database. Just as we did with the hierarchical model, we can firstly implement the model as completely different sets with all the drawbacks we noted previously.

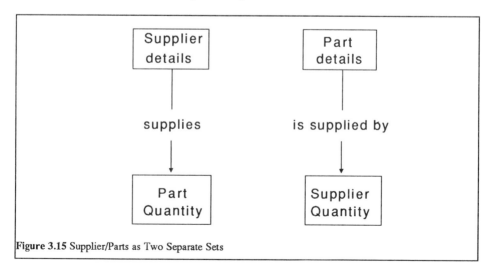

Figure 3.15 Supplier/Parts as Two Separate Sets

Such simple sets are in fact, created by linking all participating records by pointers. Taking our Supplier set as an example, we could have a structure as illustrated in Figure 3.16 below:

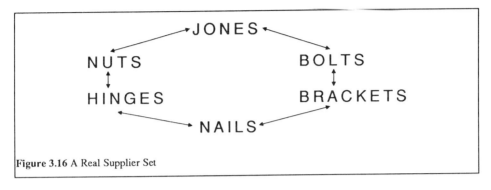

Figure 3.16 A Real Supplier Set

However, because sets can contain different types of records with pointers defining different types of relationships, we can combine our Supplier and Parts sets with the actual pointers defining who supplies what and what is supplied by whom. So let's see how such a structure can be implemented by pointers to illustrate different sets sharing, and therefore relating, different record types and occurrences. Let's use our previous example:

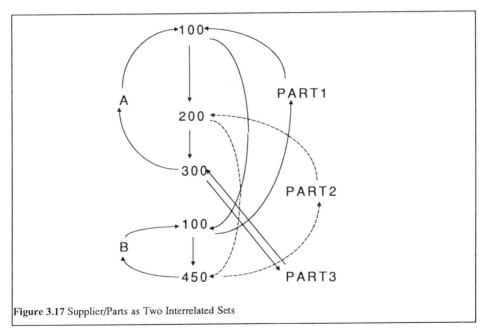

Figure 3.17 Supplier/Parts as Two Interrelated Sets

Now if we wanted to know how many part 1s are supplied by Supplier A, using Figure 3.17 above we can see that there is only one record in both the Part 1 and Supplier A set and that is 100. Looking at this simple diagram more carefully reveals

37

other interesting features. As I have already mentioned, order is inherent in the member records of a set, and the ordering is implemented by forward pointers in this example.

The arrows in Figure 3.17 all represent these forward pointers, and you might imagine that the intersection QUANTITY data probably uses more space holding pointers than it does data. This situation is made worse when you consider that it is common for such members to carry backward (prior) pointers as well, and in the extreme they also carry a pointer directly to the owner record. This pointer space is doubled for every set the record participates in, so it should no longer be a mystery why network databases got their name and their reputation, as being inflexible due to their heavy pointer orientation.

Having examined some of the logical and physical aspects of the network structure it's worth taking just a brief look at how the database is managed.

As we have seen before, there is a distinction in this model between the physical and the logical and, similar in concept to the hierarchical type, the physical database is again defined by a schema, created by COBOL-like code. Such code defines:

❏ The schema name (one per database)

❏ The record type names and their field definitions

❏ The sets and the record types that comprise the owners and members and such information as to the uniqueness of the members and their order.

As mentioned, this schema description is defined in code similar to COBOL but named DDL (Data Definition Language) by CODASYL. At the logical level and again similar to the hierarchical scheme, when an application program uses a CODASYL (network) database it must use it through a view of the data, called a sub-schema which is granted and created by the DBA. Typically such a sub-schema would be defined by extending the native COBOL language to include the required definition statements. Each sub-schema is initially provided by the DBA, and is made available by its redefinition in the application to provide correct matching to local names and storage structures etc.

In the last two sections describing hierarchical and network databases, I have gone to some length to present structure as understandably and simply as possible. The differences between the two types, and the relevance of the differences, might still not be clear, and for anyone who wishes to delve deeper, I suggest that they must seek this detail elsewhere. There are several excellent books on the subject, many of which are referenced in this text.

It is almost always the case that the best solutions are simple ones and in the database world the best solution should be a database that is easy to understand, easy to modify and can therefore be responsive to change. It is certainly true that the structures so far described offer no such advantages and in terms of flexibility. Even though to some extent they both display separation between physical and logical layers of structure, it must be stressed that few of these pointer-driven products allow either the user or DBA to change logical 'views' of current data without a great deal of effort. The effort required is invariably so prohibitive that such changes are not usually attempted. However these problems have not yet taken into account the access methods required to retrieve data from these traditional data structures which simply magnify their inflexibility.

Access Languages

Let us briefly consider another angle that I have only touched upon as yet. In the introduction of this book I paralleled the advance of database technology with that of the advancement of the computer languages that communicate with them, and just as an aim of the relational database is to be, conceptually at least, simple, then the languages that are used to access relational data must reflect this simplicity, and, of course, reflect the inherent flexibility of the database. In short they should be 'non-procedural'.

So, to state the case bluntly, there is no point in having a database structure that is flexible, if any change to such structure immediately invalidates the applications software that runs against it. This means that complexity must be removed from traditional application languages. Let us take, for example, a straight serial file on a magnetic tape and imagine we are going to read its contents, and display them on a screen.

Traditionally we would need some type of language statements, as illustrated below:

```
Open tape file
loop read record at end go to exit
     display record
     go to loop
exit close tape file
stop run
```

Such a language is termed 'procedural' in that detailed instructions are required to guide every step in performing the required function. Into this bracket we can certainly put most of the common computer languages including COBOL, FORTRAN and BASIC – a list that includes many of the languages used to communicate with non-relational databases. In contrast to the procedural approach it would be very nice and extremely productive to be able to perform the same activity with just a single command such as:

```
Display all from tape
```

This would seem much simpler and in reality the computer ought to have the intelligence to make the connection between the non-procedural command given above and the procedural steps required to execute it. It should know more about tape decks than we do. The point to this is that a 'flexible' database can only exist if it is accessible by methods that are understandable, high level, and non-procedural.

We must strive to achieve a situation whereby if data structures are added, new relationships formed, or data types changed, applications programs have some degree of protection, and will not require wholesale modification. This of course is a tall order and requires that at least two principles are adhered to:

❏ The layered database approach, already defined, is a real one, giving clear distinction between physical structures, the presentation of data to the user, and the detailed machine interface.

❏ The statements accessing the database directly, use only logical structures in a non-procedural way.

Before illustrating how the relational model satisfies these requirements let us look closely at the second of the above requirements, and examine how traditional database access is in fact wholly procedural (and thus inflexible).

Take for example a simple tree or set:

Let's give it some data:

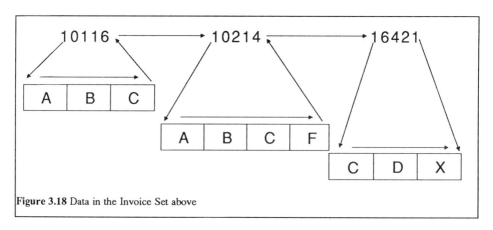

Figure 3.18 Data in the Invoice Set above

Typical language statements available to the non-relational database language for accessing such data are termed navigational and in broad terms translate to the following type of functions:

get unique	to retrieve a named record
get next	to read the next occurrence
get next down	to read the first child record
go up	to return to the parent
replace	once position has been obtained perform an update
insert	once position has been obtained perform an insert
delete	once position has been obtained perform a deletion

Thus, it is the programmer's responsibility to navigate around the data structure by using explicit commands to get the next record in sequence or move down a layer of the database hierarchy. In the rather limited example above, to retrieve all details about Invoice number 10214 we might have to code the equivalent of this:

'Get Unique'	Invoice number 10214
'Get Next Down'	to retrieve detail 'A'
'Get Next'	to retrieve detail 'C'
'Get Next'	to retrieve detail 'D'
'Get Next'	to retrieve detail 'F'
'Go Up'	to return to the parent
'Get Next'	to read the next Invoice

Of course this example exaggerates the real problem but dependence on such procedural access methods has many consequences:

❏ Programmers need an intimate knowledge of the database.

❏ Programmers need to be highly skilled and specialised.

❏ Any changes to the data structure will involve change in the applications code using them.

All three of these consequences are highly undesirable and it is only by moving away from pointer- to data-oriented database structures that we can realise both dreams of flexibility and accessibility. This is a dream answered best, although not wholly, by the Relational Database.

Summary

1) In order to truly understand the concepts and advantages of a relational database, it is necessary to understand both the strengths and weaknesses of its predecessors.

2) Most of the weaknesses of the traditional types of DBMS lie in their insistence on using physical pointers to define logical relationships. This leads invariably to complexity and inflexibility.

3) Key database advantages include ease of understanding, flexibility and accessibility. Network and hierarchical schemes are notoriously poor in all these fields, but it is these areas that will contribute most to increased productivity.

4) Flexibility in the DBMS requires flexibility in the software accessing it and so goes hand-in-hand with non-procedural and fourth-generation languages.

References

C.J. Date, An Introduction to Database Systems, 4th ed. *Addison-Wesley*, 1986.

Smith and Barnes, Files and Databases: An Introduction *Addison-Wesley,* 1987.

C.J. Date, Database: A Primer *Addison-Wesley,* 1984.

Information Management System/360 Version 2 Application Programming Reference IBM Form No SH20-0912

4

The Relational Model

There are many texts around today that adequately explain the concept and mathematics of the relational model. Such texts may go into the intricacies of set theory (set here refers to the mathematical term not that described previously as the fundamental building block of a network type database) and demonstrate quite clearly how the relational model can be proven as a logically correct way to store data.

I prefer another way of pointing out both the detail and the reasonable-ness of the model in a more pragmatic and data-oriented way. In this chapter I hope to explain the basic concepts of the relational database by describing how a data model might be formulated to take advan-tage of relational features. To understand the relational model it is important to be aware of how it originated, and how this itself puts it apart and above many other DBM systems.

Horses for Courses

Primarily, and as I have already intimated, Database Management Systems were devised and implemented to help solve specific applications problems, and because they proved successful in doing so, they were extended to provide general support to other types of application. As their generalisation increased, so their applicability, suitability, and success decreased. If we take an example from the programming world we understand clearly that whilst it is certainly possible to write simple scientifically oriented applications in COBOL, you can't hope to achieve the same degree of effectiveness as you might when using the language for a large-scale commercial batch update application. The saying 'horses for courses' is extremely pertinent to this argument, but the truth is that the relational model which spawned the RDBMS was not applications motivated. Rather it was driven from a sound basis of mathematical theory which has enabled databases based on the model to be entirely driven from natural relationships inherent in data, rather than processing concerns.

Relational databases are 'data driven' and their success depends on sound enterprise-based data analysis. However, having said that, don't for a minute think that data has any intrinsic value of its own, because it hasn't. Its value lies only in its usefulness and its ability to be turned into information. It is in this context that I have choosen to use data analysis to underpin a description of the relational database.

In the last few years and going hand-in-hand with relational ideas, the study of data normalisation has come back into increasing favour. Some see it as a true data analysis tool, whilst others use it primarily to validate the correctness of logical data models derived by other means. One way or another however, it has become recognised as a very powerful tool in the armoury of the analyst. This book is certainly not about data analysis, and it has so far implicitly presumed a certain awareness of concepts such as logical and physical database design. However the relational database model, and the art of Third Normal Form data analysis, are so intimately connected that, in simply running through a stepped approach to logical data modelling using TNF, I hope that the relational architecture will become apparent.

Let's imagine firstly that we have been given a simple business problem, and we wish to analyse it; and if it is suitable, to build a database system to handle it. To begin our analysis we might choose a methodology based on three principles outlined below:

❑ Identify the *entities* participating in that part of the real world you are trying to model

❑ Identify the *attributes* of each entity, especially those that constitute the primary identifier of each entity occurrence.

❑ Identify the *relationships* existing between the Entities.

There is an alternative idea, that data items exist as free-floating elements in a sea of information, which the analyst gathers together into relations using normalisation techniques. This leads to interesting results of which only some bear significance to the real world!

After undertaking such activity we should have identified most of the data 'objects' that are of importance to our enterprise, and how each relates to all others. Now the problem is to discover how these objects should be grouped to the maximum benefit of users, designers and programmers. As already mentioned there are many methodologies to help in this, but I am going to illustrate the method of Third Normal Form analysis as it embodies many relational principles in its methodology.

Third Normal Form Analysis

Let us illustrate the method of TNF with a further simple example. Suppose we have been asked to analyse a small system that records information about people allocated to projects. During our analysis we identify various attributes concerning this enterprise. These include:

Project code
Project type
Project description
Employee number
Employee name
Employee grade
Salary scale
Date employee joined project
Allocated time of employee on project

We might have identified these items of data, from paper forms in current use for allocating people to projects, or by other traditional and necessary methods such as questionnaires and interviews. In such a simple case it is fairly clear that we are holding data about two major entities, namely **projects** and **employees,** so it may seem reasonable to split the entire data content into two groups reflecting this idea. We might thus be tempted to implement a database as two tables so:

```
PROJECTS
PROJCODE
PROJTYPE
PROJDESC
```

```
EMPLOYEES
EMPNO
EMPNAME
GRADE
SALSCALE
DATAJNDPROJ
ALLOCTIME
```

Careful inspection of these two tables reveals that there is no connection between an **employee** and a **project** inherent in the data itself, and so to model our system might require pointers between the two to show how records in each relate to each other.

The question remains however, is this solution the correct one? To discover the answers to this we could apply TNF analysis techniques.

If we take our initial 'un-normalised' data we might identify the following values of the attributes named above.

Table 4.1 Un-normalised Project Data

PROJ CODE	PROJ TYPE	PROJ DESC	EMPNO	EMPNAME	GRADE	SAL SCALE	DATEJND PROJ	ALLOC TIME
001	APP	LNG	2146	JONES	A1	4	011176	24
001	APP	LNG	3145	SMITH	A2	4	021076	24
001	APP	LNG	6126	BLACK	B1	9	021076	18
001	APP	LNG	1214	BROWN	A2	4	041076	18
001	APP	LNG	8191	GREEN	A1	4	011176	12
004	MAI	SHO	6142	JACKS	A2	4	011177	6
004	MAI	SHO	3169	WHITE	B2	10	021177	6
004	MAI	SHO	3145	SMITH	A2	4	021276	6

Let us ask ourselves what would be the consequences of implementing our database as a single file, reflecting the above un-normalised data. There is obviously an immediate advantage in as much as the design is very simple. However if we did implement our system as a single file we will face some severe problems:

❑ Data redundancy – **Project Type** and **Description** are unnecessarily repeated many times. Clearly this is a waste of space.

❑ An **Employee** can't logically exist unless he is assigned to a **Project** – in the real world this is clearly not true.

❑ If a **Project Type** changes, many records will require updating in an identical manner.

❑ If employee SMITH gains a promotion many records will require updating.

❑ If management decides to change the relationship between **Grade** and **Salary Scale** then many updates will be required.

It seems therefore that there may be some better way to structure our database.

At this stage let us introduce some terms and ideas pertinent to normalisation. Let us refer to the above un-normalised table as a *relation* containing *columns* (representing attributes) and *rows* (each one being a record).

A first task is to select a *primary key* from the above list of columns and this key (which can comprise a number of concatenated columns) must be *unique* in that each occurrence must identify one, and only one, row in the relation. This is a relational rule – every row in a relation must be different in terms of data, than any other row; and following directly from this is the requirement that every row does, in fact, have a unique primary key.

The terms 'functional dependence' and 'transitive dependence' express the relationship between these primary key values, and the values in the other columns of a relation; both terms have important implications for normalising data. Any non-key value in a column should be functionally dependent on the primary key value. This means that if you know a primary key data value, there can only be one value for any of the non-key columns. In our example, if we accept that PROJCODE is likely to be the primary key, then PROJTYPE and PROJDESC for example, are functionally dependent on PROJCODE because for Project 001 there can only be one value for both PROJTYPE (APP) and PROJDESC (LNG).

The values in a column are transitively dependent on the primary key values if they are both functionally dependent on these values as well as on the values in another column, provided that the second column is also functionally dependent on the primary key. This sounds complicated but an example should clear up the problem. If we had chosen EMPNO as our primary key, then both SALSCALE and GRADE would be functionally dependent on it. However, in this example SALSCALE is also functionally dependent on GRADE and so we can say that SALSCALE and GRADE are both transitively dependent on EMPNO. Simple isn't it?

Let us now use these definitions to go through first, second and third normal form analysis using our hypothetical data and for each one define a simple rule, and a method and then show the results.

Firstly let us state again our un-normalised data:

PROJ CODE	PROJ TYPE	PROJ DESC	EMPNO	EMPNAME	GRADE	SAL SCALE	DATEJND PROJ	ALLOC TIME
001	APP	LNG	2146	JONES	A1	4	011176	24
001	APP	LNG	3145	SMITH	A2	4	021076	24
001	APP	LNG	6126	BLACK	B1	9	021076	18
001	APP	LNG	1214	BROWN	A2	4	041076	18
001	APP	LNG	8191	GREEN	A1	4	011176	12
004	MAI	SHO	6142	JACKS	A2	4	011177	6
004	MAI	SHO	3169	WHITE	B2	10	021177	6
004	MAI	SHO	3145	SMITH	A2	4	021276	6

First Normal Form

Rule   A relation is in First Normal Form if the intersection of any column and row contains only one value.

Method   Identify a suitable primary key from the pool of un-normalised data.

Remove any items that repeat within a single value of this key to another relation bringing with them the primary key to form part of a new composite key in the new relation.

In our example, for a given PROJCODE which we can reasonably identify as a primary key, several items repeat namely:

EMPNO
EMPNAME
GRADE
SALSCALE
DATEJNDPROJ
ALLOCTIME

What we are looking for in this type of activity is the fact that there can be many **Employees** working on one **Project** for example. By implementing this rule therefore, we end up with a new relation giving two relations in total. This new relation will have a composite primary key of PROJCODE/EMPNO.

| Result |

PROJCODE	PROJCODE
PROJTYPE	**EMPNO**
PROJDESC	NAME
	GRADE
	SALSCALE
	DATEJNDPROJ
	ALLOCTIME

(Note: **PROJCODE** bold in both boxes, **EMPNO** bold)

Second Normal Form

Rule A table in FNF is also in SNF if the values in every column are functionally or transitively dependent on the complete primary key.

Method For every relation with a single data item making up the primary key, this rule should always be true. For those with a compound key, examine every column, and ask whether its value depends on the whole of the compound key or just some of the parts of it. Remove those that depend only on part of the key to a new relation with that part as the primary key.

Result Our relation defined by PROJCODE is already in SNF so we can disregard it for the moment. However in the second relation that we created by applying the first rule of TNF, we can see that a person's name depends only on part of the key, that part in this case being EMPNO. Clearly a person's name does not change depending on what project he is assigned to. Therefore applying the SNF rule we now end up with three relations.

PROJCODE	PROJCODE	EMPNO
PROJTYPE	EMPNO	NAME
DESC	ALLOCTIME	GRADE
	DATEJNDPROJ	SALSCALE

Third Normal Form

Rule A relation in SNF is also in TNF if the values in every non-key column are not transitively dependent on the primary key.

Method Examine every non-key column and question its relationship with every other non-key column. Ask the question, if I know the value for column 'A', is there only one value for column 'B'? If the answer is 'yes', remove both columns to a separate table and mark the unique one as the primary key.

Result   Suppose in our example we have a situation where a particular
GRADE supports three different SALSCALEs as represented in
Figure 4.1 below:

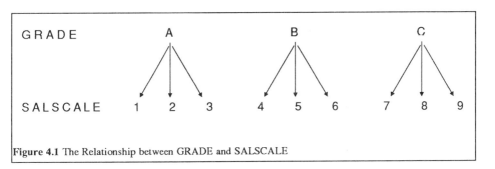

Figure 4.1 The Relationship between GRADE and SALSCALE

If we ask the question: for GRADE A is there only one possible value of
SALSCALE? then the answer is clearly 'no' because the allowable values are 1, 2 or
3. However if we reverse the question and ask: for a SALSCALE of 2 is there only
one possible GRADE? then the answer is now 'yes' and we have discovered a
transitive dependence between GRADE and SALSCALE. Because of this relationship
both columns are carried forward to a new relation and the most selective column
appointed the status of primary key within the new relation. This new primary key
must be left in the original relation as what is termed a foreign key. We now have
four relations representing our original un-normalised data in Third Normal Form.

PROJCODE PROJTYPE PROJDESC	**PROJCODE** **EMPNO** DATEJNDPROJ ALLOCTIME	**EMPNO** NAME GRADE	**GRADE** SALSCALE

This thumb-nail sketch of Third Normal Form analysis shows us how to organise our
un-normalised data into a data model and we can show this now as a logical data
model complete with relationships.

PROJECTS Projcode Projtype Projdesc	**EMPLOYEES** Empno Name Grade	**GRADES** Grade Salscale	**ALLOCATION** Projcode Empno Datejndprj Alloctime

Figure 4.2 A Logical Model Of Our Project Allocation System

This model should be implementable in a Relational Database as a set of tables, with a guarantee that not only is each table related to others by the sharing of common columns (attributes), but that the data is held with minimum duplication and that some degree of flexibility is present. Now let's revisit the problems that were identified in our un-normalised data:

1) The first problem we noted was that of data redundancy and it is tempting to think that relational databases encourage such redundancy because they require duplicated data in order to define relationships. Do not be drawn into this false way of thinking because such data is *not* redundant and in nearly all cases a RDBMS manages data more efficiently regarding space and redundancy than other types.

2) The existence of an **Employee** now requires no relationship to a **Project** so we can easily add new **Employee** details to our **Employee** table whether he has been assigned to a project or not. We have in effect created a personnel table.

3) If a **Project Type** changes, only one record requires updating.

4) If SMITH gains promotion, again only one record requires updating.

5) If the relationship between **Grade** and **Salary Scale** is changed only the few records that explicitly specify these relationships require modification.

The reason why I have preceded talking about the relational database model with this introduction of TNF should now become apparent because:

❏ A relational database is one that can directly support, at the logical level, a data model in TNF.

❏ Relations can map directly to database Tables.

❏ Attributes can map directly to table Columns.

❏ The TNF concept of a primary key is directly supported in the RDBMS.

❏ The concept of the relationship between primary and foreign keys is fundamental to the relational 'JOIN' operator. We shall come back to this later.

Of course this is not a complete picture of the relational concept, but in the real world it is a useful view point as it shows clearly the potentially direct relationship between the entity, attribute relationship model producible from business analysis, and the tables, columns, primary and foreign key concepts crucial to the relational database. I do not wish to give the impression that TNF analysis is a technique used only in connection with relational design. In fact it is a strong analysis tool whichever way data is to be organised, but it is certainly true to say that a relational database is the only one that can directly support a data model defined in terms of the TNF rules.

Turning TNF Output into a Relational Database Model

As I have stressed, it is possible to take the TNF relations we have defined for our 'Projects' database, and implement them directly in an RDBMS, with each relation mapping directly to a table, with a column representing each of the attributes. In a system where performance is not critical, this would be a highly desirable state of affairs because it maximises simplicity and flexibility.

To expand on this last point let's examine the SQL required to change our logical data model into a physical database under some sort of generalised RDBMS. In terms of activity we would need to:

1) Create a database

    CREATE DATABASE PROJECTS;

2) Define the four tables

CREATE TABLE PROJECT	(PROJCODE INTEGER, PROJTYPE CHAR(9), PROJDESC CHAR(100));
CREATE TABLE PAYSCALE	(GRADE CHAR(2), SALSCALE CHAR(2));
CREATE TABLE EMP	(EMPNO INTEGER, NAME CHAR(100), GRADE CHAR(2));
CREATE TABLE ALLOC	(PROJCODE INTEGER, EMPNO INTEGER, DATEJNDPROJ DATE, ALLOCTIME INTEGER);

3) Specify the primary keys as indexes

    CREATE UNIQUE INDEX ON PROJECTS(PROJCODE);

    CREATE UNIQUE INDEX ON EMP(EMPNO);

    CREATE UNIQUE INDEX ON ALLOC(PROJCODE,EMPNO);

    CREATE UNIQUE INDEX ON PAYSCALE(GRADE);

4) We may feel the need for secondary indexes

    CREATE INDEX ON EMP(GRADE);

Foreign keys are often good candidates for secondary indexes although in this case the volumes of data involved would probable not warrant the inclusion of an index.

51

5) And we may like to add some security features (here we're giving everyone access to everything!)

GRANT ALL ON ALL TO ALL;

Having done this we have largely completed the job, and our database is ready to receive data! I should stress however, that we have not at this stage build a separate and distinct logical layer because it would, in this very simple case, closely reflect the physical layer. This is not always the truth by a long way, but it is rare, in real life to see applications talking solely through views, and it will be a little while before the value of doing so is universally understood and accepted.

Two Vital Relational Concepts Revisited

Before moving from the subject I would like to reinforce two of the more critical aspects of the relational model which, although they have been covered elsewhere, deserve to be stressed again at this point.

1) Relational databases do not allow repeating groups. To be precise, data values are atomic, meaning that at the intersection of a column and row there will never be more than one value.

Therefore a COBOL type record:

03 Field 1
03 Field 2 OCCURS 3

looking something like this:

Field 1	Field 2 (1)	Field 2 (2)	Field 2 (3)
JOB	SALES	MARKETING	ADMIN

will be represented in a relational model as three records (rows):

Field 1 **Field 2**

JOB	SALES
JOB	MARKETING
JOB	ADMIN

2) The entire data content of a relational database is represented as explicit data values. This means that there are no 'links' or pointers forming the logical structure of the database and that all relationships between data items exist purely by way of the values of these data items.

Because this factor is the most crucial of the whole relational world I am going to emphasise this with another example to illustrate it. Along the way we'll go through TNF again and see how an Entity Attribute Relationship (EAR), model can be implemented in relational terms.

Let's proceed therefore with the Supplier/Parts example that was used previously. Going back to a previous diagram (Figure 3.7 on page 32) we have a many-to-many relationship between the entities PARTS and SUPPLIERS. Let us suppose we identify the following attributes within our example:

Supplier No
Supplier Name
Quantity
Part No
Part Name.

This then is our un-normalised data.

If we should select **Supplier No.** as the primary key for this data set, we can proceed to normalise it using TNF analysis techniques.

First, by removing the repeating groups we go to FNF.

Un-normalised   **FNF**

Supplier No		Supplier No		Supplier No
Supplier Name		Supplier Name		Part No
Part No				Part Name
Part Name				Quantity
Quantity				

We then look at relations with compound keys to examine the data for 'part key dependencies' thus proceeding to SNF.

SNF

Supplier no		Supplier No		Part No
Supplier Name		Part No		Part Name
		Quantity		

By examination we confirm that this data is in fact in TNF as well, so by adding some entity (table) names, our final model can be represented as below.

Supplier		**Part**		**Supply List**
Supplier No		Part No		Supplier No
Supplier Name		Part Name		Part No
				Quantity

We would then implement this in our relational database as:

```
CREATE TABLE SUPPLIER            ( SUPPNO INTEGER,
                                   SUPPNAME CHAR(20));

CREATE TABLE PART                ( PARTNO INTEGER,
                                   PARTNAME CHAR(20));

CREATE TABLE SUPPLIST            ( SUPPNO INTEGER,
                                   PARTNO INTEGER,
                                   QUANTITY INTEGER);

CREATE UNIQUE INDEX INDONE ON SUPPLIER(SUPPNO);

CREATE UNIQUE INDEX INDTWO ON PART(PARTNO);

CREATE UNIQUE INDEX INDTHREE ON SUPPLIST(SUPPNO,PARTNO);
```

What we now have is two straight lists of all our **Suppliers** and all our **Parts**, and an up-to-date listing of who supplied what and in what quantity. If we progress to putting some data into the tables we can illustrate how our two relational rules are in fact in force.

SUPPLIER	PART	SUPPLIER LIST
1432 JONES	4 NUT	1432 4 1000
1564 PAGE	10 BOLT	1432 10 4000
1724 FLUX	13 HINGE	1432 13 650
1841 WINDWARD	6 SCREW	1724 4 204
1324 JAMES	2 RIVET	1324 6 650
		1324 4 700

Figure 4.3 A Simple Supplier/Parts Database

We can clearly see that at any intersection of columns and row there is only one value, and we can also see that the relationships existing between **Supplier** and **Part** are maintained purely by the data content of the Supplier list table. If for example the row 1324,4,700 is deleted from the Supplier List, then the relationship between **Supplier** JAMES and the **Part** NUT is extinguished – there is no need to delete physical pointers or reorganise any data because the relationship is defined purely in terms of data held in the tables.

Relational Structures

Let's now take a closer look at the relational database in terms of its structure in the hope of finding out just why it has become so popular.

The relational database provides the clearest distinction yet between the three layers of a database that I have so far been at such great pains to describe. The implementation of the different layers has each brought its own significant advantages and these layers can be clearly illustrated as in Figure 4.4 below:

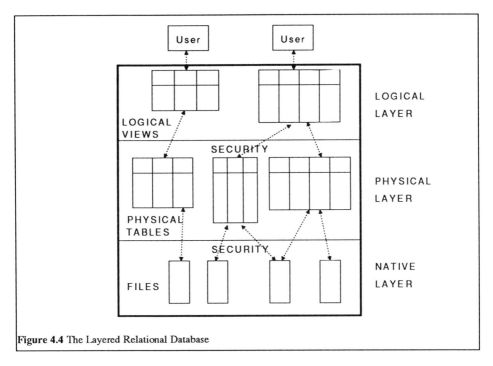

Figure 4.4 The Layered Relational Database

At the physical level the database is constructed as a set of two-dimensional tables which consist of *columns* and *rows* – these correspond directly to the more common concepts of *fields* and *records*.

Tables are maintained by the RDBMS which, invisibly to the user, maps them to the native operating system in whatever record management facilities the vendor of the RDBMS prefers in that native environment. Ingres on the VAX VMS system for example, uses the RMS record management facility to support its tables and just how it does so is largely unimportant to us.

The logical layer of the database is constructed of *views* which can be thought of as windows onto the physical database. Views are defined in much the same way as tables and are best thought of as logical tables each defined on one or more physical tables.

Thus we have a system where:

1) The business model is reflected in views at the logical level (sub-schemas).

2) Physical tables are created by the DBA, and form the foundation of the required Views. They are representative of the logical model, but need not be replications of it (schemas).

3) The RDBMS manages the physical tables it terms of the native operating systems record management facilities, transparently to the user.

I am fond of the term map because you can think of the user peering through a View which is in effect a map of one or more tables. These tables themselves are maps of physical storage, so in effect the user perceives data that passes through at least two levels, where it can be invisibly changed (or remapped) as it travels from disk to user.

Relational Operators

In order to qualify as 'relational' in even the most basic way, a DBMS must support the concept of tables, and data must be held in nothing else but this form. In addition, and in order to provide for access to data from such tables and to build logical structures on them as described above, the DBMS must also provide support for a fairly closely defined set of operators. It is usual for this support to come from an implementation of SQL but this is certainly not mandatory. Included in this set of operators are the following:

JOIN

Used to connect data from one or more tables by relating the contents of columns which have an equivalent meaning (are drawn from the same domain).

TAB1				TAB2				Result		
A	B	C		D	A	E		A	B	E
1	2	s		e	1	4		1	2	4
2	f	g		p	2	x		2	f	x
x	e	5		7	x	q		x	e	q

```
SELECT TAB1.A,TAB1.B,TAB2.E
     FROM TAB1,TAB2
        WHERE TAB1.A = TAB2.A;
```

Note here that if there is no WHERE clause an operation called a *Cartesian product* will occur in which every row from one table will be joined from every row in the other. For example:

```
SELECT * FROM TAB1, TAB2;
```

will yield:

A	B	C	D	A	E
1	2	s	e	1	4
2	f	g	e	1	4
x	e	5	e	1	4
1	2	s	p	2	x
2	f	g	p	2	x
x	e	5	p	2	x
1	2	s	7	x	q
2	f	g	7	x	q
x	e	5	7	x	q

PROJECT

Used to select a subset of columns from the total available.

TAB1		
A	B	C
1	2	s
2	f	g
x	e	5

Result	
B	C
f	g
e	5
2	s

SELECT B,C FROM TAB1;

RESTRICT

Enables the selection of specific rows from the total available.

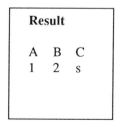

TAB1		
A	B	C
1	2	s
2	f	g
x	e	5

Result		
A	B	C
1	2	s

SELECT * FROM TAB1 WHERE A = 1;

UNION

Brings back data from more than one table without the need for join; usually when all tables are modelling the same type of entity.

TAB1		
A	B	C
1	2	s
2	f	g
x	e	s

TAB2		
A	B	C
e	1	4
p	2	x
7	x	q

Result		
A	B	C
1	2	s
p	2	x
7	x	q
x	e	s
2	f	g
e	1	4

```
SELECT A,B,C FROM TAB1
UNION
SELECT A,B,C FROM TAB2;
```

INTERSECT

Returns only those rows that are present in all nominated tables.

TAB1		
A	B	C
1	2	s
2	f	g
x	e	s

TAB2		
A	B	C
e	1	4
1	2	s
7	x	q

Result		
A	B	C
1	2	s

```
SELECT A,B,C FROM TAB1
INTERSECT
SELECT A,B,C FROM TAB2;
```

MINUS

Returns only those rows from a table that are not present in other nominated tables.

TAB1		
A	B	C
1	2	s
2	f	g
x	e	s

TAB2		
A	B	C
e	1	4
1	2	s
7	x	q

Result		
A	B	C
2	f	g
x	e	s

```
SELECT A,B,C FROM TAB1
MINUS
SELECT A,B,C FROM TAB2;
```

DIVISION

This operation is not currently supported in SQL but should return rows from the dividend table which have occurrences matching all those in the divisor table.

TAB1		TAB2	Result
A	B	A	A
1	2	e	x
2	f	q	
x	e		
x	q		
2	q		

We should have noted by this stage, some fundamental differences between the relational database and its forerunners; and the following table should serve to summarise some of these.

Table 4.2 Differences between Relational and Non-relational

Non-relational	*Relational*
Relationships maintained by pointers	Relationships defined purely by data content
Access to data through predefined paths	Any data item is always directly addressable
Structural changes very difficult if not impossible	Very flexible at logical level
Inherently complicated data structures	Conceptually simple data structures
Ordering of records significant	No significance in order of rows
Accessing programs require procedural and navigational capability	No such restrictions
	Supported and maintained by a standard set of operators

In essence, the fundamental difference that sets the relational database apart from others, is that it was designed as a general purpose facility from a sound theoretical basis, and is not in any way applications oriented. Many people use this fact to deride the architecture in the same way you might use the saying 'a Jack of all trades but master of none', but as the relational product line improves in quality, we will find them to be the equal or better of other types of data management facilities.

Summary

1) The relational database seeks to ensure that all occurences of data and the relationships between them are defined explicitly and visibly. This sets it apart from all other systems and is a major advantage.

2) In order to succeed it relies on the inherent structured nature of data which is often revealed by such techniques as Third Normal Form data analysis.

3) Data structures in TNF can be implemented directly by a relational database but because of other factors, this is rarely seen in the real world. It does however, represent a significant advantage.

4) Just as a relational database demands structure, it also demands set-based operators to access data in a structured manner.

References

Peter Chen, The Entity-Relationship Approach to Logical Database Design, *Wellesley, Mass. Q.E.D. Information Sciences*, 1977

R. Veryard, Pragmatic Data Analysis Oxford, U.K. *Blackwell Scientific Publications*, 1984

T DeMarco, Structured Analysis and System Specification, New York *YOURDON Press*, 1978

James Martin, Computer Database Organisation Englewood Cliffs, N.J. *Prentice-Hall*, 1982

Shaku Atre, Database: Structured Techniques for Design, Performance and Management, 2nd Edition *John Wiley*, 1988

Sitansu S Mittra, Structured Techniques of Systems Analysis, Design and Implementation *John Wiley*, 1988

C Fleming and B von Halle, Handbook of Relational Database Design *Addison-Wesley*, 1989

5

Relational Database Architectures

Having examined the logical structure of the relational database, and delved into the types of operations it supports it's time to examine how it works as an item of software. As to be expected, the actual workings of an RDBMS are quite complex in terms of which software components perform which function, and different architectures have been favoured in different products. The discerning technician may manage to isolate areas where one product scores over the other in terms of the way in which certain features have been implemented. However the products themselves are evolving quite quickly, and most have changed shape dramatically as they have sought to increase performance to preserve competitiveness.

This chapter is primarily concerned with how the RDBMS sits on a machine in terms of the process structure it requires and what might be the case in the future.

Relational Database Aims

A few years ago, when the relational revolution was just the twinkle in the eye of one or two vendors, the most important driving force was to market a product that worked. Nowadays the emphasis on working has diminished in importance as the products have matured and been proved successful, to be replaced by other factors. Three important aims have now emerged:

❑ Performance

❑ The ability to distribute data

❑ The ability to handle enormous quantities of data

All vendors are currently seeking solutions to these problems and these are not easy tasks by any means. Oracle for example required major parts of its internal structures to be rewritten, to ease the bottleneck caused by its single database server architecture; whilst Ingres, originally blessed with the opposite problem, has performed similar surgery aimed at reducing the number of processes required to support an installation. Such changes are far from trivial however, and represent major investment for the vendors with the accompanying risk. Many people will remember that when relational databases first came to the market the opinion of most commentators were that such databases were inherently slow. This was not true. The apparent slowness that was witnessed was not a problem of the concept, but rather a reflection of the fact that at the time performance was not an issue so little investment was spent in that area. Vendors at that time were too busy making their products work and adding functionality to be concerned with performance alone.

However, it is enough to say that originally many different types of process architecture came into being, and now there is a realisation that there are possibly only a small number of architectures that can provide effective solutions to the three problems above. In many ways we are witnessing at the moment, a move from many diverse architectures toward these ideal models.

The picture is therefore one of change and so there is little point in this book of detailing architectures which may be out of date at any moment. Having said this however, once again, Oracle and Ingres in versions up to six of each, are quite different, and worthy of some discussion, especially when considering how their designs may change in the future.

It is important to understand how an RDBMS works in relation to both the data itself and the user community it services because different methods are better suited to different solutions; it is true that some RDBMSs can offer a preferred solution to certain types of users and hardware environments.

The Server Architecture

One thing that most relational database implementations do share, and is as good a place to start as any, is what is known as a server architecture between cooperating processes. This means that the processes serving the application, or perhaps communicating with the user – the 'front end' – will be different from those that talk directly to the database – the 'back ends' – and there will be some sort of communications or service between the two types of process. In reality there are three types of server architecture illustrated currently in relational database products.

The Single Server Architecture

In this system, all users have their own process to manage their communication with the database, but all these front ends communicate to the database disk subsystem through a single database server process, which provides a central service for interpretation of SQL requests and all disk I/O – there is a single 'back end'.

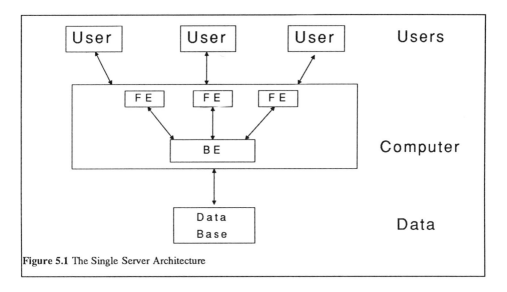

Figure 5.1 The Single Server Architecture

The One-To-One Client/Server Architecture

This architecture is characterised by the fact that each user has both a dedicated front-end process and database server process.

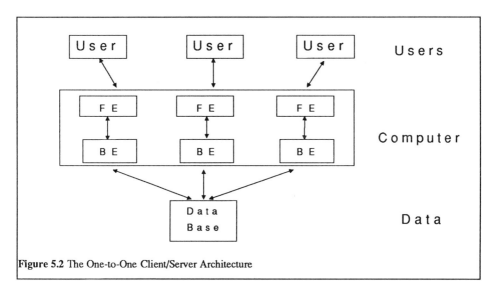

Figure 5.2 The One-to-One Client/Server Architecture

The Multiple Server Architecture

Again each user has his own front-end process, but the number of back-end processes is now configurable by the system manager or Database Administrator to best suit the load and available hardware.

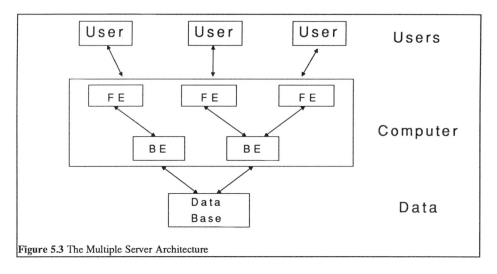

Figure 5.3 The Multiple Server Architecture

Based on these skeletal architectures many alternatives are possible, but before discussing individual examples, let us examine the important features of these simplistic schemes, and thereby perhaps learn some of their advantages against the perhaps more obvious single process per user architecture.

Firstly, I don't think it is too difficult to accept that, when a user executes a query on data held in a database, there are indeed two very different sorts of activity required. To provide the user with an acceptable environment to allow him to construct the query, may require code to accept input from a terminal, and display output in a pleasing format. Typically such interaction with the user is performed by what I have termed up to now, a 'front-end' process, of which there will usually be one per active user. One function of this front-end, as already stated, is to handle the input and output (I/O) with the user, but a second is to pass on the SQL statement representing the query that the user wishes to execute, to a database server process that I have termed the 'back-end'. This process needs to know nothing about how that SQL came about but simply to recognise that it exists and to execute it, and pass the result set back to the user. Now let's make some pertinent points about this type of architecture.

1) Generally there will be one front-end process for every user logged on to the database through any utility or application. These processes will generally utilise any memory-sharing mechanisms provided by the operating system, and may represent a *bona fide* application, a report generator or perhaps an SQL monitor. The object of the front-end is to communicate the user's requirements to the back-end in the form of an SQL query, and to interpret the results from such requests in a format suitable to the user or application.

2) Talking directly to the database will be any number of back-end processes, and these basically are responsible for the following activities:

❑ Syntax checking of the SQL passed by the front end processes

❑ Parsing the SQL requests

❑ Validating the request by checking for the existence of named objects and checking access rights etc.

❑ Quering optimisation.

The back end will also be responsible for all database read and write activity and for maintaining any other file structures required for the correct running of the database (logging files, journalling files etc).

3) Some type of fast communication will be required between front-end processes (the clients) and their appropriate back ends (servers). Such communication will be typically implemented in shared memory facilities such as VMS mailboxes, the contents of which will usually be SQL requests or data parcels.

4) The clean divide between front- and back-end processing facilitates distributed processing architectures.

5) Because instructions from the front end to the back end are coded in a universally accepted language (SQL), it should be possible for a single front end to talk to different types of relational database.

6) The fact that only the back-end processes talk to the physical database enables some optimisation to better suit this software to differing hardware platforms.

It seems therefore that there are several compelling reasons to maintain these client/server process architectures and, bearing this in mind, let's take time to outline some of the current implementations of the strategy.

The Oracle Architecture

Let us first consider the Oracle (Version 5) process structure:

When an Oracle installation is first defined, a utility called CCF is used to create two files, the database file and the Before Image (BI) file. These files have a fixed length at creation time, so some thought needs to be given to their intended use; a job which needs a certain amount of planning. The database file itself can later be extended by creating further 'files' and it is possible this way to distribute the database over more than one disk drive. The Before Image file cannot be extended this way.

After these files have been created and initialised, a program called IOR (Initialise Oracle), is executed for that particular database. Termed 'warm starting Oracle' this program has several functions:

❑ to open the database file(s) and BI file

❑ to roll back any transactions that were uncompleted during the last session

❑ to initialise various memory areas

❑ to start four other detached processes

When the IOR program finishes, Oracle will, to all intents and purposes, be available for users to logon and, alongside any user-processes created by such logon activity, the four processes mentioned above should also be active. Under certain operating systems the 'father' process of these four, IOR itself, will also still exist, although it will contribute nothing further until the system shuts down when it is again activated. Note here that in such operating systems one must be careful not to abort IOR as this may well cause the failure of its 'sons' – the detached processes. Under these conditions the database will fail, with the loss of any non-committed transactions.

The four processes function in direct support of the database, and run even if there are no users logged on. They are termed 'server' processes and perform all write access to the database and BI file on behalf of any user process. In our previously introduced terminology, these four detached processes together constitute the 'back-end' database server process. In fact this type of architecture is peculiar to Oracle, and is rather different from that situation where a single back end is capable of performing all database functions. The way Oracle works therefore, is in simplistic terms as a single back-end system, although this 'back end' does consist of more than one process.

A single implementation of an Oracle database, therefore, consists of a defined area of 'data space', a predefined Before Image file, a Kernel of software performing caching and optimisation, amongst other things, and four separate processes used by all users to perform certain specialist tasks. All users also own a front-end process, which manages their communication with the database itself, and this is done by passing requests (queries) or data to and from this front-end process and the caches maintained by the central kernel (in particular, the part of the kernel called the System Global Area (SGA)).

All parsing, access checking and optimisation for example, are performed by this central kernel software, but all requests to write data physically to the database are passed from the kernel to the Buffer Writer process, which again is a single process serving all users. When data is requested by a user with the intention of modification, a copy of that data in its unchanged form is written to the Before Image file by the single Before Image Write process, and this allows the old data to be written back to the database should either the user change his mind and abort his update or a system failure occur. It also allows people to read the old copy of data that is currently being updated.

The processes that write to the database and the Before Image File are two of the 'detached processes'. There are two others and the following paragraphs summarise the functionality of the detached processes in general.

Asynchronous Read Ahead (ARH)

If a user query is likely to require a full scan of an entire table, ARH is invoked to copy not one, but several contiguous pages of data at a time, into a global cache area, in the hope that it will thus have pre-empted the next read request from that user.

This can speed up such queries significantly as ARH can be retrieving data whilst the user program continues processing it, and is especially pertinent in systems that physically store data in key order. Indexed reads are performed directly by the user process and thus bypass ARH.

Before Image Writer (BIW)

The Before Image Write process is the only process that writes to the Before Image file. When a user starts to update a page of data, the BIW will write a copy of that page before it is modified to the BI file. This ensures its original state is kept safe, in case it needs to be reapplied to the database later because the update fails for some reason. If such a condition does arise then on restarting Oracle (or aborting a transaction) relevant pages of data still active in the BI file are applied to the database, neatly 'rolling back' all transactions that did not successfully complete. The BI function also services read requests that are made on data already selected for update because that read activity can be diverted from the database pages themselves to the BI copies.

Buffer Writer (BWR)

BWR is the process that writes to the database files. When a user commits changes made to data pages in memory, BWR is activated and transfers that data from memory to the physical database tables, at the same time writing any After Image journals if this facility is in use.

Clean Up Process (CLN)

This process cycles at intervals removing all traces of 'dead' processes from memory and/or database structures.

To put all this in context the following block diagram illustrates the Oracle structure.

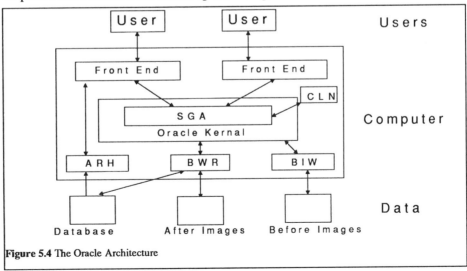

Figure 5.4 The Oracle Architecture

To see how it all works, let us imagine that a user logs onto a database to do an update to a specific data row, and that After Image Journalling (AIJ) is active. Let's break down the job into steps roughly in time sequence, in order to illustrate the contributions of the different components. There is a detailed description of After Image Journalling in Chapter 15, but in simple terms, it is a method of logging a completed transaction for security purposes.

The sequence of events for the update activity are:

1) The Oracle database is 'warm started', which is a privileged job usually performed once at the start of the day. Any outstanding Before Images are reapplied to the database, to bring it into a consistent state – these may exist because normal database processing was aborted for some reason, at the end of the last session. The BI file is initialised and the four detached processes are created.

2) The user logs onto the database, thus creating a front-end process of his own through which to work.

3) The user formulates an SQL command to do the update, either at a terminal session, or perhaps by parameters input to an application running as the front-end and this SQL is passed to the Oracle kernel software (shareable code containing the query logic) to be parsed, optimise and executed.

4) The required data row that is to be updated is fetched from the database into the data buffers of the SGA, and a copy of it is also written to the BI file by the BIW process. The data row is locked against any other user attempting to update or delete it.

5) The data row is passed, or made available, to the application where it is changed by the user.

6) When the update is committed (the user is satisfied with it and decides to go ahead and action the update), either implicitly or explicitly, the BI of the transaction will be marked as redundant, and the BWR process will write the updated data page to the database and to the After Image file, thus ensuring that the data change has been recorded in the physical database.

7) The next cycle of CLN will ensure that all traces of the transaction are removed from any memory buffers used, and all outstanding locks are dropped.

8) At the end of the day when all users have logged off, the system will be 'shutdown', and from then on be out of service until the next warm-start.

It should be appreciated that the above is intended to outline the mechanisms only, and the actual details may differ slightly. The important points to note in this type of architecture are that:

❑ The back-end comprises different types of processes, which each occur once per database.

68

- There is little direct communication between front-ends and the I/O processes, especially the database writes.

- There is one SGA per database, and this mechanism is a shared memory resource for all uses of the database. It holds system-wide buffers and intelligence, and is tunable by many system-defined parameters.

Before leaving this architecture let me highlight some of the good and bad points that you may have noticed:

- The Before Image process, by holding the old version of any data currently undergoing update, enables both the system, or an individual user, to cancel a transaction at any stage, by writing the old copy of any changed data over that changed copy. The user can activate this by issuing a ROLLBACK operation at any stage in a transaction, and if the system should fail, it will automatically abort all transactions and roll any half-completed transactions out on the next 'warm start' using this Before Image facility.

- After Image Journalling is optional, and ensures that the results of all transactions that have been successful, are recorded on some media (typically tape) other than the database itself. This facility offers protection against gross failure of the database.

- The retention of BI copies of data currently being changed, enables the system to allow read activity against such data. The data in its changed form will not become readable to other users until commit time.

- This architecture keeps much of the major activity of the database centralised and thus lends itself to the criticism of bottle-necking particularly in terms of database I/O.

The Ingres Architecture

The Ingres solution (version 5) in essence seems much more simple but in fact provides much the same functionality.

Firstly, there is no concept in this system of warm starting the database because if any database is not actively being used, then there will be no processes associated with it. The architecture, in fact, seems to encourage the creation of multiple databases, in direct contrast to Oracle, and these databases are static, inasmuch as they do not support any associated 'detached processes' as does Oracle. This factor is important because we must remember that, for every Oracle database, there will always be four server processes active, and therefore the presence of many databases will quickly use system resource, even if there are no active users. As stated, Ingres almost encourages the creation of multiple databases (the reasons why this is so should become evident later) and this is aided by the fact that there are no central database server processes contributing to the back-end overhead, but rather every user that uses a database creates, not only a front-end process in which the application runs, but also a dedicated back-end server which handles all database activity on behalf of that specific user. Unless a user logs on to a database, the Ingres installation uses no memory or CPU resource, and there is therefore a clear difference in this type of architecture from that illustrated previously, which is rather surprising really as they both do a similar thing for similar people on the same type of machines.

So lets us examine the Ingres architecture more carefully, using some of the terminology I have already explained. A user running an Ingres-based application, or any of the development tools available, will run the program in a front-end process. As this process is created, it will spawn its own dedicated back-end process, and communications between the two will be managed by whatever facilities the native operating system provides. Typically the front-end function is to interpret user activity, and convert this into commands that will be understood by the RDBMS, and then to pass these commands to the back end for execution. Similarly, results will be retrieved by the back end from the database, and passed to the front end, to be interpreted and displayed to the user.

Imagine, for example, that a user is running an application which displays a screen on which he can query data. Imagine also, that he formulates a query on this screen and decides to execute it. The chain of events will be:

1) The front-end application may perform some sort of validation of screen input.

2) The front end will formulate the query in terms of SQL and 'post' this command to its back end. This posting mechanism may be akin to the mailbox facility supported by DEC's VMS operating system for example, or some other memory sharing device.

3) The back-end process (which is simply a program supplied with Ingres), then performs several tasks on behalf of the query:

   ❏ The 'syntax checker' will check the syntax of the command.

   ❏ The parser breaks the query into data structures and operations, and builds a 'query tree'.

   ❏ Any query modification is performed on the query tree, including any additions necessary due to the existence of integrities, permissions or the use of views etc.

   ❏ The query optimiser ponders over possible execution plans, arriving at the most efficient one.

   ❏ The query is executed.

4) The data resulting from the query is obtained from the physical database, or local and global memory caches and returned to the front-end process.

5) The back-end process will also handle any locking or journalling requirements.

Comparing the two approaches

In my two descriptions of Oracle and Ingres, I have taken a different stance for each, thus avoiding direct comparison. I justify this position because of both the speed at which modifications are made to these architectures, and the difficulty (and perhaps irrelevance) of obtaining detailed, current and lasting information. To illustrate this we need look no further than the Query Optimiser. Whilst we know that all RDBMSs will have some software driven mechanism for optimising queries, (and I will take some time to expand on this later), the level of usefulness and intelligence of this facility are major areas constantly targeted for improvement. I have not mentioned the Oracle Query Optimiser but it certainly exists, and one can guarantee, especially in the world of distributed databases, that the vendors leading the field in their ability to significantly improve query optimisation, will have tremendous advantages. It is not easy to get detailed information on those areas that are potentially market winners.

Up to this point I have explained the working of Oracle and Ingres Version 5, and the most obvious factors when distinguishing the two are that:

❏ Ingres supports multiple back ends, one for each user.

❏ Oracle has what is in effect a single back end for all users of the same database. This back end is capable of multi-tasking/processing, and so avoids bottle-necks where and when possible. Disk I/O is off-loaded to separate processes, which can run logically in parallel with each other and query processing.

❏ The nature of Ingres leads to the evolution of many discreet databases, where Oracle seems to favour the larger centralised multi-purpose database approach.

❏ Each Ingres user has his own transient journal to enable roll-back of uncompleted transactions. This is a centralised function within Oracle.

It is an interesting fact that perhaps the two best known mini-computer-based Relational Database Management Systems have chosen, at least up to their Version 5 releases, two radically different methods of implementing their systems. It's hard to believe that both systems can be optimal and in fact the move of the two products into the high-performance arena has required modifications to both, as illustrated in the next chapter.

Summary

1) Fully functional RDBMSs perform a great deal of activity on behalf of their user community and, as time goes by, this functionality will be increased in order to relieve the burden from the applications shoulders.

2) There are many different ways of implementing an RDBMS, and Oracle and Ingres have chosen architectures very different to each other. Whilst both separate

the user process from the RDBMS engine, there are many significant differences, each carrying with them good and bad points.

3) The split between front- and back-end functionality is absolutely essential in order to allow greater performance and distribution of processing. It seems that an architecture allowing multiple and configurable back-end database server processes will be favoured, and certainly both Oracle and Ingres are being modified to fit this type of strategy.

References

Date and White, A Guide to DB2, Second Edition *Addison-Wesley*, 1988

C.J.Date, A Guide to Ingres *Addison-Wesley*, 1987

Stonebraker, The Ingres Papers: Anatomy of a Relational Database Systems. *Addison-Wesley*, 1986

J Aaron Zornes, Sequent/Ingres Performance Report – The Silver Bullet Benchmark *Relational Technology Inc.*

6

On-Line Transaction Processing

As I've mentioned previously, early implementations of relational database systems were considered to be too slow for any form of 'real time' activity, and were generally seen as more suited to flexible report-based systems, or ones with low activity. Due largely to the progress of the Sybase product, and the various manoeuvrings by IBM in the positioning of DB2, enormous performance improvements have been witnessed, both on the software and hardware fronts, and at last RDBMS vendors are preparing themselves for the push into the multi-million pound market of On-Line Transaction Processing.

Principles of Transaction

Those of you not familiar with the idea of a transaction, or moreover its fundamental use in defining a 'unit of work', should consult Chapter 11 before proceeding further. Those who are still with me will recognise that a transaction can include a work load ranging from an update of a single row of data controlled by a single SQL statement, to very complex update activity indeed, including update, insert and delete from multiple tables controlled by many interrelated SQL statements. In the world of a consolidated database which serves all company needs, there will be a variety of types of units of work being executed against the database at any time, and these can largely be divided into three categories:

❏ On-line transaction processing (OLTP)

❏ Batch update

❏ Management Information systems (MIS)

The first and third of these types of work are fundamental to data processing activity, but the second can be thought of as existing for expediency sake only. I therefore propose to leave this type of processing out of further discussion, after pointing out that, in a fully integrated data processing environment, the need for it should be hugely reduced as on-line update and data centralisation becomes more sophisticated. In fact, as data architectures become more elaborate, companies may well find that batch update runs practised currently become impossible in the future. Of course, certain types of batch update activity will be a requirement for some companies for many years. However it is still justifiable to relegate its importance, because it will more closely come to resemble multiple on-line transactions executing against data concurrently, rather than the complex activity which so commonly requires specialised recovery routines and the database dedicated to itself.

Fundamentally, the difference between OLTP systems and information systems are ones of scale, criticality and function. In terms of OLTP, the major function is as a front-end application being used to gather data and keep it up to date whilst the information systems use this up-to-date data to create up-to-date information.

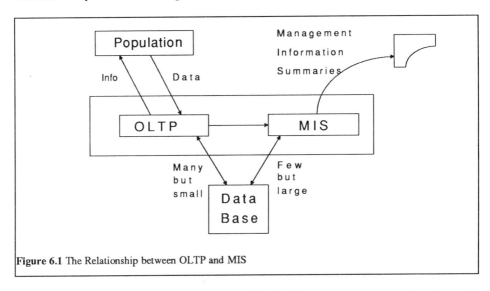

Figure 6.1 The Relationship between OLTP and MIS

Let us see how this works by considering Mr Smith who has a complaint about his telephone bill. Mr Smith is a member of our 'population' above and to satisfy his query he may telephone his complaint to a British Telecom (or AT & T perhaps) employee on the complaints desk. He may be asked, amongst other things, his name and address, and maybe even his reference number, and with this information the person manning the complaints desk, with the aid of a terminal, will quickly be able to retrieve to his screen the full account details of Mr Smith.

Hopefully, by examining the data retrieved, any error will be identified and corrected there and then 'in real time', and the corrected data recorded in the Accounts database. Thus the computer application used at this stage is termed as an on-line transaction processing system and demonstrates some of the characteristics of such systems:

❑ It is on-line and immediately available

❑ From small amounts of key data it can retrieve larger quantities of related information

❑ It allows data update in 'real time'

❑ It is critical to the business

❑ It has clearly defined functions

❑ The complete transaction starts and finishes in a single time frame.

Although Mr Smith will now be contented that the error has been discovered and rectified, the incident is not yet over. Typically we will expect at least two further actions. At some later stage a new statement must be despatched to Mr Smith and it is also likely that some type of report of the incident will be produced for management. Later this same billing data may be incorporated into all sorts of other sales-related information grouped perhaps by geographical areas, product types or population classes, and it is these types of information systems which form the second type of transaction. These are characterised by the facts that they:

❑ Are less time critical

❑ Create printed output

❑ Read large quantities of data to produce summarised output

❑ Are often 'read only' and therefore need no complex restart procedures

❑ Are usually heavy resource users in terms of CPU and I/O

❑ Are variable in requirement.

There are therefore, fundamental and easily identifiable differences between OLTP-type applications and information system applications on a theoretical basis, but in fact a large number of systems fall in between the two. Indeed many applications will have functions falling into both categories, and typically these types of systems have been termed 'hybrid' – although this is not a term I like to use.

The factor of 'scale' allows us to examine the distribution of systems as to their transaction nature. Typically an OLTP system will support the execution of many simple and similar transactions concurrently, whilst a non-OLTP system will execute a small number of large transactions. Thus the number of transactions per second that an application system is required to support can be used to measure whether it can be defined as an OLTP system. A typical distribution is shown in Figure 6.2 on the next page.

While users see that rapid response to customer requests is an essential competitive weapon the need for high performance on-line applications will continue to grow dramatically. Whilst at present the majority of on-line systems require TPS rates of less than 30 or so, in 1987 alone the OLTP market was estimated to be worth close to $20 billion worth of hardware and software, and geared to double by 1991.

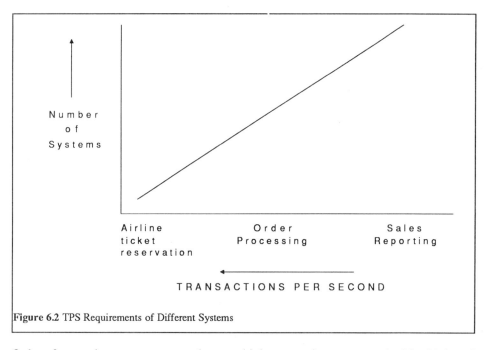

Figure 6.2 TPS Requirements of Different Systems

Only a few environments support the very high transaction rates required by high-end OLTP applications. IBM offer its specially sculptured Transaction Processing Facility and its IMS/Fastpath product, Tandem offers VLX Non Stop SQL, and Teradata offers the DBC/1012 as perhaps the only truly relational offering capable of very high rates of transaction throughput.

As I have already mentioned, relational database management systems were often berated as being slow, and it is for this reason that they have not yet infiltrated the OLTP market. They certainly will do so soon, and at this time the following notable products are being directed this way with some determination, and can already process transactions at a 'reasonable rate':

IBM DB2   the aim is to replace IMS

Oracle V6   in conjunction with the TPS module

Ingres V6   including Silverbullet technologies

Sybase   designed from the start to support OLTP

Teradata DBC/1012   massive parallelism gives nearly unlimited capability

Tandem VLX   running non-stop SQL, many fault tolerant features

Hopefully the days when organisations, wishing to develop systems with high transaction throughput, had to forsake such relational advantages as flexibility – ease of use and portability are on the way out and RDBMSs will be able to handle requirements across the board of TPS ratings.

OLTP Characteristics

So what is it then that characterises the database that is to support high transaction rates? There are perhaps five characteristics that such a DBMS must have:

1) The *sine qua non* of an OLTP system is to be able to **sustain high transaction throughput rates.**

2) Because OLTP systems are usually critical to the business they drive, they must be completely trustworthy in both the **integrity of the data** they hold and the **functioning of the hardware.** Some degree of fault tolerance will be a requisite, as will be **comprehensive recovery facilities.**

3) An OLTP system must be able to grow to support large applications in a **predictable and acceptable fashion.**

4) The system must provide for **scalable performance** gains per unit of increased hardware power.

5) An OLTP system must have **high availability** provided by the fact that all parts of all transactions are executed in real time thus avoiding batch type updating.

In terms of workload it is also clear that the requirement is for a relational DBMS with, in addition to the facilities mentioned above and elsewhere in this text, the ability to support mixed work loads, whether they be transaction or *ad-hoc* in nature. To do this, vendors are looking both at hardware and software as areas for performance improvements.

Hardware Solutions

A key challenge to today's RDBMS vendors wishing to move their products into an OLTP marketplace, is to fully utilise the multiple processor hardware technology that is becoming so common nowadays. Already many hardware vendors are marketing machines with more than one tightly coupled processor and these include notable products from:

❏ IBM with its 4381, 3090 mainframes

❏ VAX with the 8800 series and the newer 6200

❏ Sequent with its Balance and Symmetry range

Throughput rates are related to CPU power and so it's reasonable to suggest that the more CPU power at the DBMS's disposal the greater will be the potential throughput. Of course, with large amounts of CPU, I/O is likely to be a problem but I'll deal with improvements in this field under the software section. So where can we go to see how RDBMSs are being sculpted to utilise multi-processing capability? A good place to start is by using an example of hardware which implements multi-processing in a very loosely coupled way, and for this reason I've chosen the VAX cluster as a prime example.

In a typical VAX cluster, multiple VAX processors are linked together using a high speed bus (the Computer Interconnect or an Ethernet connection). All processors will also have further connectivity via hierarchical storage controllers to give intelligent and shared access to multi-ported disk drives.

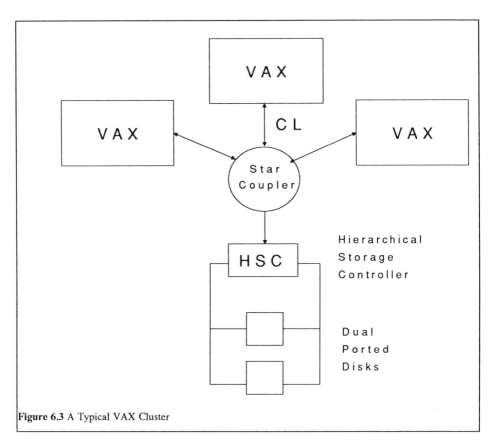

Figure 6.3 A Typical VAX Cluster

Some key advantages of this type of hardware configuration include:

❏ Shared discs

❏ Shadowed discs

❏ Data path redundancy

❏ Scalable performance

❏ Preservation of existing investment

These advantages alone add up to considerable reasons for positioning an RDBMS onto a VAX cluster to give OLTP-type characteristics. However there are other areas to be considered, perhaps the most important being the actual architecture of the RDBMS itself. Reminding ourselves of the three alternatives available, let us see what happens if we put a DBMS with a single server architecture onto a cluster (see Figure 6.4 below).

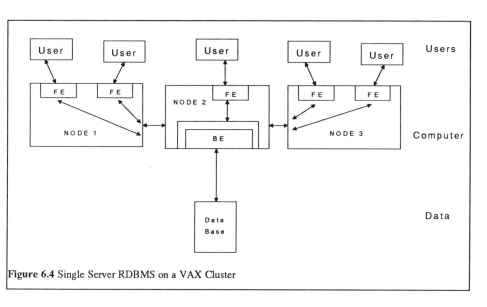

Figure 6.4 Single Server RDBMS on a VAX Cluster

In actual fact we achieve very little. Certainly we can support a large number of users on our cluster, a number which will depend entirely on the configuration of individual VAXes in the group, but there remains two serious setbacks. Firstly we have introduced a single source of failure because if the VAX that hosts the single database server (or back end) becomes unavailable, so will the whole database installation. Secondly, no degree of scalable performance is attained because the requests and data of all users must pass through the single back end which effectively bottle-necks throughput. In tightly coupled multi-processor environments the problems remain, and it seems unlikely that this simple software architecture has a glowing future.

If we look at the architecture that provides for one back-end process for every front end (Ingres Version 5 for example) we can certainly achieve multiple-processor advantages but at a considerable waste of resource, so I'll skip over this and move to what seems likely to be the real solution, namely the multi-server database architecture, which will allow the number of servers to be tuned to the hardware environment. (See Figure 6.5 on the next page).

Under this scheme each node in a cluster (or processor in a mainframe) can host a database server process each of which can service one or many user front-end processors. Such an architecture provides for:

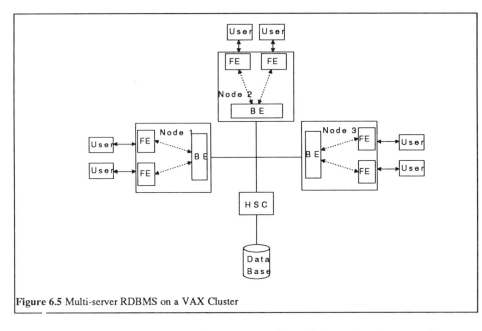

Figure 6.5 Multi-server RDBMS on a VAX Cluster

Scalability	processors and servers can be added to give linear performance increases.
Fault Tolerance	if one processor goes down, all functions of the database system can be preserved on other processors for all users.
Tunability	the different servers residing on different processors can be assigned different priorities, loadings and work mixes.

So by selecting the correct combination of multi-processor hardware and RDBMSs with multi-server architectures, many of the requirements for OLTP can be met. However, beware of one or two things:

1) Some products started their life as single-server systems and have been patched to better exploit multi-processor hardware. Some of this patchwork has not been particularly successful.

2) The addition of extra processors to some computers, does not give linear performance increases by a long way, because such machines have yet to implement operating systems that can schedule multi-processors effectively. Figures have been published that indicate that the addition of a fourth processor to a VAX 8800 machine may realise just 18.5% of that processor's power, even under versions of VMS supporting Symmetric Multi-Processing.

3) Each user, even in a multi-processor environment, will usually get the service of only one processor at one time – and this could be as little as a Intel 80386 processor in the Sequent machines for example.

Software Solutions

So far we have examined the ways in which hardware can help to provide for the high throughput requirement of OLTP, by allowing the simultaneous execution of many processes within the confines of a single processor complex. Certainly the VAX cluster is a specialised type of multi-processor, but many of the concerns and advantages reflect those that one would expect in tightly coupled systems such as found in the Sequent machines. However, not only is it possible to attain higher throughput with hardware solutions; significant performance increases have been attained by software improvements based, in the main, on reducing I/O. Most vendors, it must be said, have chosen the same few software enhancements to increase performance, and it's certainly worth looking into some of them more closely.

Compiled Transactions

The age-old argument concerning the merits of compiled against interpreted code were bound to catch up with the relational world sooner or later, especially with SQL being such an obviously interpreted language, and it's true again, that compiling SQL queries can be expected to contribute to greater performance. In reality, the meaning of 'compiled' might not be what you expect, and it usually means that the Query Execution Plan (QEP – see Chapter 10), which is a definition of the low-level actions necessary to execute an SQL command, are saved in the data dictionary, rather than being discarded on the completion of every SQL command. When a user executes an SQL command, part of the RDBMS evaluates the best way to perform it, and produces an execution plan as a set of actions, executes these actions and then discards the plan. Unfortunately, if the user then types the same SQL command, albeit with different data, then the QEP needs to be recreated (it will usually be the same, of course) and this is clearly a waste of time under most circumstances. Compiling an SQL statement, or more usually a transaction, ensures that the QEP is retained and therefore removes the need for it to be re-evaluated time after time and, in an OLTP environment, where the transactions are usually predefined and optimised, such facilities can be a great benefit.

Most systems implement some type of facility in this area but there are dangers. An advantage of using interpreted SQL is that the actioning of each SQL command is optimised every time, based on the data content and structure of the database at that instant. If we compile an SQL statement which retrieves data from an unindexed column for example, then even if we add a useful index at some later stage, this particular query will not use it until it is recompiled.

Multi-Volume Tables

It's only recently that some software based RDBMSs have been able to spread single tables over multiple disk drives and in fact, even now, only the better ones support this facility. This is a shame because it allows two things which are critical to OLTP environments. Firstly such ability allows the support of large tables – those that will simply not fit on one disk, and secondly the benefits of utilising more than one controller concurrently when responding to a single query, will facilitate a degree of parallelism in I/O operations, which can help throughput by both hastening read and write activity and reducing contention. A little later in this book we will see how the splitting of tables across large arrays of disks can lead to enormous processing advantage, a technology that is advancing very quickly at the moment.

Deferred Write

One of the most productive ways of gaining performance is to cut down physical I/O to the database. A favourite method is simply to store as much changed data as possible in memory, in order to write it out in batches when the machine is not so busy; or even better, to avoid writes altogether. In essence this is the 'deferred write'. Let's illustrate this by using what we already know about Oracle version 5 and comparing it with version 6 of the same product.

When a user of version 5 Oracle updates data, he incurs three types of disk I/O. Firstly a copy of the data to be updated is written to the Before Image File. Secondly as the changes are committed, the changed data is written to the database and thirdly, if chosen, that same changed data is written to the After Image file. In a complex transaction this can add up to a great deal of disk activity. Version 6 addresses this problem in several ways. To start with the BI write is dispensed with, and while pages of data are being changed in memory their old images are retained. Secondly, on a successful commit, the changed pages are not written directly to disk, but instead entries recording those changes, in a compressed format and on a multiple user basis, are written to the Redo log.

Thirdly, as an independent asynchronous process, the Redo log is archived to a permanent dataset to provide for after imaging. In addition, and again as an asynchronous process, changed memory pages are applied to the database on a least recently used basis.

Such architectural changes preserve data integrity and save, or take off-line as it were, a great deal of I/O activity. Let's look at these three I/O saving techniques to see how they do in fact preserve integrity.

Firstly, the saving of the before images of changed data in memory retains the ability of a user to read data that is currently undergoing change. Secondly, because the changed images are available in memory for further processing there is no need to apply them directly to the database as long as the changes are recorded to disk in the Redo log. If the machine fails, thus wiping out the memory-based changes, the Redo log is applied to preserve the integrity of the database. Thirdly, a permanent method of rolling forward a database from a checkpoint is available, because all the successful changes have been permanently recorded from copies of the Redo log.

There are therefore some fundamental I/O saving techniques and these same facilities, in different flavours, are utilised in all the products aimed at OLTP type markets – compare for example Ingres's Fast and Group commit concepts.

To summarise so far, we can see two separate approaches to solving the problem of providing high transaction throughput in the RDBMS. One is to utilise CPU in a more effective manner, and the other is to reduce I/O to a minimum but safe level. The other major resource in a computer is memory, and implicit in what has so far been discussed are two methods of better utilising this resource:

❑ Moving away from the one back-end/one front-end architecture conserves memory, otherwise wasted by being allocated to non-productive processes.

❑ Deferred write allows memory to be used in a purposeful and safe way.

Most RDBMSs will also support a variety of cache management systems, which improve throughput by retaining often used items of data or code in fast access memory thereby effectively reducing the total I/O activity of a database. Common targets for caching are parsed SQL statements, Query Execution Plans, data, index pages or dictionary contents, and such caches are often tunable in size, and most often are managed on a least-recently-used basis.

In general, caches are only useful if the same data is being used continually either by the same user or by different users. Their usefulness is also diminished by the fact that, as a cache is expanded in an attempt to make it more beneficial, the mechanisms of actually accessing the cached data will slow to a point where it may be quicker to go to the actual disk copy. Remember also, that true, system-wide caching will not be available on multi-processor systems that do not have shared memory – VAX cluster for example.

The Benefits of Parallelism

It is tempting to call the type of multi-processing that I have so far referred to, as parallel processing, and to some extent it is just that. Certainly many processes serving many different users can be active concurrently, and this is largely what parallel processing is all about. On a single-user basis however, there is little perceived advantage because the user can only get full use of a single processor at any one time, so is there an alternative?

SQL itself is what we call a 'set based' language in that no single command can be executed against a single row of data, but rather every command will act on all rows which qualify as targets of that command – the target set. This target set can be as little as a single row, or as much as every row in a table, but the actual fact is that every row that qualifies in the target set, will be processed in exactly the same way as any other. This fact makes SQL a prime language to support parallelism in ways aimed at providing single users with massive simultaneous processing power.

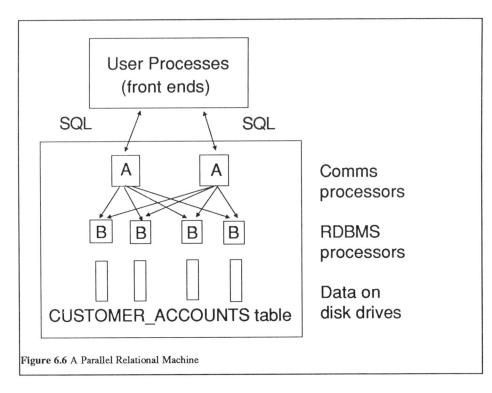

Figure 6.6 A Parallel Relational Machine

Let's look at the computer shown in Figure 6.6.

Each lettered box represents a processor and, spread across the four disk drives, let's imagine we have a one million row Customer Account table. Each drive will hold 250,000 rows of this table and is each managed by a single processor (B). To see how true parallelism can work (in fact this schema is representative of the Teradata DBC/1012) let us imagine our user enters the SQL command from a front end process:

SELECT SUM (ACCOUNT_TOTALS) FROM CUSTOMER_ACCOUNTS;

Generally (on other types of architecture) this will require a full table scan of every row in the table to compute the sum required as the answer, and let us say this takes 400 seconds. On our architecture depicted above, once processor A has parsed the SQL, it can pass it simultaneously to each B type processor which now only has to scan through 250,000 rows to find the total for its subset of data. Of course, all B type processors can scan their rows in parallel, so the total time to completion using this type of hardware will be a quarter of the 400 seconds mentioned earlier. This then represents a considerable improvement, but if we had a computer with 1,000 or so type B processors, we could expect an elapsed time of around one thousandth of 400 seconds or in other words, very quick indeed.

As I mentioned earlier, when discussing the drawbacks of multi-processors, if on this type of parallel machine, a user inputs a command of the order:

```
SELECT ACCOUNT_TOTAL FROM CUSTOMER_ACCOUNTS
   WHERE CUSTOMER_ACCOUNT_NO = 178293;
```

then the time to execute will be that in which a single type B processor can retrieve the qualifying row from its disk, and the immediate advantages of the parallelism is lost to this user. However this architecture can support many users performing such queries concurrently because, more often than not, each query will be executing on a different type B processor, so no contention will be occurring, and the throughput can be enormous.

The above solution demands much investment because it requires both specialised hardware and software, and is solely dedicated to the single task of database management and access. Not many systems require the huge power of such machines, and in general it is now proving possible to buy a solution fitting every problem and every pocket, with the mediating factor that at present the following requirements are likely to cost a lot of money:

❏ Large amounts of data

❏ Fast access

These two characteristics nearly define the world of OLTP, and I find it hard to believe that RDBMSs without the aid of specialised hardware, will be able to make an impact on this type of market.

Summary

1) Systems supporting OLTP-type activity are fundamentally different to the information systems for which they provide data.

2) Databases supporting OLTP need sophisticated functionality, unwarranted in MIS only systems. The goal must be, however, to have a single RDBMS capable of supporting the whole range of applications activity.

3) Whilst the OLTP market is currently considered to be quite small, it is projected to be a huge source of revenue for the RDBMS vendors. It's reasonable to expect a great deal of effort to be put into developing products to support these types of applications, in the near future.

4) It's unlikely that purely software-based solutions will be capable of supporting very high transaction per second ratings – so look toward specialised hardware, especially the database machines, incorporating micro-processor technology and disk arrays.

7

When is a Database Relational?

Many database products on the market today claim to be 'relational' and these include both those that have some justifiable claim to do so (Oracle, DB2 and Ingres for example) and those that have merely implemented a relational 'look' to their non-relational product (Adabas, IDMS/R, ADR Datacom).

There is a common trend of thought with regard to this second class of products, that if a DBMS looks or behaves like a relational one to the end-user, then indeed it can be said that it is relational.

This idea should be treated with a great deal of suspicion and I prefer the more rigorous definition of the relational model based on the 12 rules first published in Computer World in October 14 and 21, 1985, and devised by the renowned E Codd. For the sake of completeness, this chapter describes these rules, and tries to put some practical meaning behind them, so that they might be used to throw more light on relational products, or those that claim to be.

Relational Definition

In the most basic of definitions a DBMS can be regarded as relational only if it obeys the following three rules:

❏ All information must be held in tables.

❏ Retrieval of this data must be possible using the following types of operations:

SELECT
JOIN
PROJECT

❏ All relationships between data must be represented explicitly in that data itself.

This really is the minimum requirement, but it is surprising to see just how some well-known database products fail according to these simple rules to be in fact, relational, no matter what their vendors claim.

To define the requirements more rigorously, compliance with the 12 rules stated below must be demonstrable, within a single product, for it to be termed 'relational'. In reality it's true to say that they don't all carry the same degree of importance, and indeed some very good products exist today supporting major large-scale production systems that cannot, hand on heart, claim to obey any more than eight or so of these rules. It's likely however, that it is only when all 12 rules can be satisfied, by facilities that coexist together, that the full benefits of the relational database can come to fruition.

The Twelve Rules

Just as in the 12 rules that define the distributed product and are described in Chapter 18, there is a single overall rule which in some ways covers all others and is commonly called Rule 0. It states that:

Any truly relational database must be manageable entirely through its own relational capabilities.

Having stated this rule, I will not delve deeper except to say that its meaning can be interpreted by stating that a relational database must be 'relational, wholly relational and nothing but relational'. It's difficult to argue against this!

Rule 1: The information rule

All information is explicitly and logically represented in exactly one way – by data values in tables.

In simple terms this means that if an item of data doesn't reside somewhere in a table in the database then it doesn't exist and this should be extended to the point where even such information as table, view and column names to mention just a few, should be contained somewhere in table form. This necessitates the provision of an active data dictionary, that is itself relational, and it is the provision of such facilities that allow the relatively easy additions to RDBMS's of programming and CASE tools for example. This rule serves on its own to invalidate the claims of several databases to be relational simply because of their lack of ability to store dictionary items (or indeed 'meta data') in an integrated, relational form. Commonly such products implement their dictionary information systems in some native file structure, and thus set themselves up for failing at the first hurdle.

Rule 2: The rule of guaranteed access

Every item of data must be logically addressable by resorting to a combination of table name, primary key value and column name.

Whilst it is invariable possible to retrieve individual items of data in many different ways, especially in a relational/SQL environment, it must be true that any item can be retrieved by supplying the table name, the primary key value of the row holding the item and the column name in which it is to be found. If you think back to the table-like storage structure, this rule is saying that at the intersection of a column and a row you will necessarily find one value of a data item (or null).

Rule 3: The systematic treatment of null values

It may surprise you to see this subject on the list of properties, but it is fundamental to the DBMS that null values are supported in the representation of missing and inapplicable information. This support for null values must be consistent throughout the DBMS, and independent of data type (a null value in a CHAR field must mean the same as null in an INTEGER field for example).

It has often been the case in other product types, that a character to represent 'missing or inapplicable data' has been allocated from the domain of characters pertinent to a particular item. We may for example define four permissible values for a column 'SEX' as:

M   Male
F   Female
X   No data available
Y   Not applicable

Such a solution requires careful design, and must decrease productivity at the very least. This situation is particularly undesirable when very high-level languages such as SQL are used to manipulate such data, and if such a solution is used for numeric columns all sorts of problems can arise during aggregate functions such as SUM and AVERAGE etc.

Rule 4: The database description rule

A description of the database is held and maintained using the same logical structures used to define the data, thus allowing users with appropriate authority to query such information in the same ways and using the same languages as they would any other data in the database.

Put into easy terms, Rule 4 means that there must be a data dictionary within the RDBMS that is constructed of tables and/or views that can be examined using SQL. This rule states therefore that a dictionary is mandatory, and if taken in conjunction with Rule 1, there can be no doubt that the dictionary must also consist of combinations of tables and views.

Rule 5: The comprehensive sub-language rule

There must be at least one language whose statements can be expressed as character strings conforming to some well defined syntax, that is comprehensive in supporting the following:

❏ Data definition

❏ View definition

❏ Data manipulation

❏ Integrity constraints

❏ Authorisation

❏ Transaction boundaries

Again in real terms, this means that the RDBMS must be completely manageable through its own dialect of SQL, although some products still support SQL-like languages (Ingres support of Quel for example). This rule also sets out to scope the functionality of SQL – you will detect an implicit requirement to support access control, integrity constraints and transaction management facilities for example.

Rule 6: The view updating rule

All views that can be updated in theory, can also be updated by the system.

This is quite a difficult rule to interpret, and so a word of explanation is required. Whilst it is possible to create views in all sorts of illogical ways, and with all sorts of aggregates and virtual columns, it is obviously not possible to update through some of them. As a very simple example, if you define a 'virtual column' in a view as A*B where A and B are columns in a base table, then how can you perform an update on that virtual column directly? The database cannot possible break down any number supplied, into its two component parts, without more information being supplied. To delve a little deeper, we should consider that the possible complexity of a view is almost infinite in logical terms, simply because a view can be defined in terms of both tables and other views. Particular vendors restrict the complexity of their own implementations, in some cases quite drastically.

Even in logical terms, it is often incredibly difficult to tell whether a view is theoretically updatable, let alone delve into the practicalities of actually doing so. In fact there exists another set of rules that, when applied to a view, can be used to determine its level of logical complexity, and it is only realistic to apply Rule 6 to those views that are defined as 'simple' by such criteria.

Rule 7: The insert and update rule

The capability of handling a base relation, or in fact a derived relation, as a single operand must hold good for all retrieve, update, delete and insert activity.

This is fairly self-explanatory and in global terms means that the major DML commands, namely SELECT, UPDATE, DELETE and INSERT (or their equivalents) must be available and operational on sets of rows in a relation.

Rule 8: The physical independence rule

User access to the database, via terminal monitors or application programs, must remain logically consistent whenever changes to the storage representation, or access methods to the data, are changed.

Therefore, and by way of an example, if an index is built or destroyed by the DBA on a table, any user should still retrieve the same data from that table, albeit a little more slowly. It is largely this rule that demands the clear distinction between the logical and physical layers of the database that have been described in some detail in Chapter 2. Applications must be limited to interfacing with the logical layer to enable the enforcement of this rule, and it is this rule that sorts out the men from the boys in the relational marketplace. Looking at other architectures already discussed, one can imagine the consequences of changing the physical structure of a network or hierarchic system.

However their are plenty of traps awaiting even in the relational world. Consider the application designer who depends on the presence of a Btree type index to ensure retrieval of data is in a predefined order, only to find that the DBA dynamically drops the index! What about the programmer who doesn't check for prime key uniqueness in his application, because he knows it is enforced by a unique index. The removal of such an index might be catastrophic. I point out these two issues because although they are serious factors, I am not convinced that they constitute the breaking of this rule; it is for the individual to make up his own mind.

Rule 9: The logical data independence rule

Application programs and terminal activities must remain logically unimpaired whenever information preserving changes of any kind, that are theoretically permitted, are made to the base tables.

This rule allows many types of database design change to be made dynamically, without users being aware of them. To illustrate the meaning of the rule the examples on the next page show two types of activity, described in more detail later, that should be possible if this rule is enforced.

Firstly, it should be possible to split a table vertically into more than one 'fragment', as long as such splitting preserves all the original data (is 'non-loss'), and maintain the primary key in each and every fragment. This means in simple terms that a single table should be divisible into one or more other tables.

TAB1				FRAG1		FRAG2		
A	**B**	**C**	**D**	**A**	**B**	**A**	**C**	**D**
1	A	C	E	1	A	1	C	E
4	A	C	F	4	A	4	C	F
6	B	D	G	6	B	6	D	G
2	B	D	H	2	B	2	D	H

Figure 7.1 TAB1 split into Two Fragments

Secondly it should be possible to combine base tables into one by way of a 'non-loss join'.

FRAG1		FRAG2			TAB1			
A	**B**	**A**	**C**	**D**	**A**	**B**	**C**	**D**
1	A	1	C	E	1	A	C	E
4	A	4	C	F	4	A	C	F
6	B	6	D	G	6	B	D	G
2	B	2	D	H	2	B	D	H

Figure 7.2 Two Fragments Combined into One Table

Note that if such changes are made, then views will be required so that users and applications are unaffected by them.

Rule 10: Integrity independence rule

All integrity constraints defined for a database must be definable in the language referred to in Rule 5, and stored in the database as data in tables.

The following integrity rules should apply to every relational database:

❑ No component of a primary key can have missing values – this is the basic rule of **entity integrity.**

❑ For each distinct foreign key value there must exist a matching primary key value in the same domain. Conformation to this rule ensures what is called **referential integrity.**

Referential integrity has become such an issue these days that I have included a detailed discussion on it in Chapter 14. For the time being, it should be remembered that, whilst there are many aspects of data integrity, the above two rules should be seen as mandatory for any relational database.

Rule 11: Distribution rule

A RDBMS must have distribution independence.

This rule takes us into the world of the distributed relational database, and states that applications running on a non-distributed database must remain logically unimpaired if that data should then become distributed in the context of a distributed relational database. It's probably true that the relational model is the only one which has any hope of supporting this rule, because of its immense power in decomposing tables into sub-tables (fragments), and in fact recombining them with its SQL JOIN, UNION, MINUS and INTERSECT operators.

Rule 12: No subversion rule

If an RDBMS supports a lower level language that permits for example, row-at-a-time processing, then this language must not be able to bypass any integrity rules or constraints defined in the higher level, set-at-a-time, relational language.

This rule is fairly self explanatory, and is one that has 'found out' some of the products that have merely built a relational front end onto their non-relational database systems. In general, if all database access is through SQL then there should be no problem here, but certain products, of which Cullinet's IDMS/R was a notable example, did (or do) support a 'row-at-a-time' access mechanism below the relational integrity constraints interface, and thus clearly violate this rule.

The practical importance of these rules is difficult to estimate, and depends largely on the RDBMS in question, its proposed use and individual view points, but the theoretical importance is undeniable. It's interesting to see how some of the rules relate to others, and to some of the more important advantages of the relational model. It is unlikely at the present time that any RDBMS can claim full logical data independence because of their generally poor ability to handle updating through views. Even token adherence to this rule however, when combined with facilities enabling physical data independence, potentially yield advantages to applications developers, unheard of with any other type of database system. Coupling these two rules with the data independence and distribution independence rules can take the protection of customer investment to new heights.

I do not hold with the wars that have been waged concerning which RDBMS scored most points out of the 12 available, and consider those that hold this evaluation above all else are likely to be missing the point in some way. Success in the relational world comes with a mixture of experience, theory and pragmatism, but still it remains comforting to know that, whilst only time brings experience which validates pragmatism, you can have the theory 'off the shelf' today.

The beauty of the relational database is that the concepts that define it are few, easy to understand and explicit. The 12 rules explained in this chapter can be used as the basic relational design criteria, and as such are clear indications of the purity of the relational concept. Whilst you do not find these rules being quoted so often these days as in the recent past, it does not mean that they are any less important. Rather it can be interpreted as reflecting a reduced importance as propaganda. Other factors, of which performance is the most obvious, have now taken precedence.

Summary

1) There are 12 rules which define the scope and functionality of a relational database. The list is definitive and largely undisputed in the industry.

2) These rules can be used as a guide when evaluating products, or to give an insight into the concepts of a relational database; but remember that some are more important than others, in both general and specific terms.

Part 2

Relational Database Management Systems

8

SQL

We must now accept the fact that the primary access path to data held in relational databases will be through a common language called SQL or Structured Query Language. This decision has been taken out of the hands of the would-be vendor, and user and I do not wish to debate the good and bad points of this here.

When stated so starkly, this situation may seem a little bleak, but in fact this standardisation on SQL is of immeasurable benefit to all concerned. SQL certainly has many faults, and some of these are outlined in this chapter, but it is proving time and time again to be sufficient for all but the most unusual and demanding of tasks.

Rather than describing the language in any detail here, and bearing in mind that the major constructs of the language have already been covered, I would rather spend some time in this chapter dealing with some aspects of the language, and its implementation, that may be of concern or interest to the prospective user.

Why SQL is Favoured

Firstly I'd like to answer a very important question and that is: why has SQL found such overwhelmingly great favour in such a relatively short time?

Without being cynical, and pointing out the advantage of originating from within IBM, there are two major factors. Firstly, SQL is perceived as being easy to use, and secondly as being portable between different vendors RDBMSs. So let us start this chapter by examining just how true these two perceptions are.

Ease of use

SQL commands can be roughly divided into three major categories with regard to their functionality. Firstly, there are those used to create and maintain the database structure. The second category includes those commands that manipulate the data in such structures, and thirdly there are those that control the use of the database. To have all this functionality in a single language is a clear advantage over many other systems straightaway, and must certainly contribute largely to the rumour of it being easy to use.

It's worth naming these three fundamental types of commands for future reference. Those that create and maintain the database are grouped into the class called DDL or Data Definition Language statements and those used to manipulate data in the tables, of which there are four, are the DML or Data Manipulation Language commands. To control usage of the data the DCL commands (Data Control Language) are used, and it is these three in conjunction plus one or two additions that define SQL. There are therefore no environmental statements, as one finds so irritating in COBOL: for example, no statements to control program flow (if/then/else, perform, go to) and of course, no equivalent commands to open and close files, and read individual records. At this level then, it is easy to see where SQL gets its 'end-user-tool' and 'easy-to-use' tags, and whilst I am certainly not going to define the SQL language in this book, a quick run through of the types of commands available will illustrate why SQL is deemed a comparatively easy language.

The Data Definition Statements

To construct and administer the database there are two major DDL statements – CREATE and DROP, which form the backbone of many commands:

CREATE DATABASE	to create a database
DROP DATABASE	to remove a database
CREATE TABLE	to create a table
DROP TABLE	to drop a table
CREATE INDEX	to create an index on a column
DROP INDEX	to drop an index
CREATE VIEW	to create a view
DROP VIEW	to drop a view

There may be some additional ones, such as ALTER TABLE or MODIFY DATABASE, which are vendor specific.

The Data Manipulation Statements

To manipulate data in tables directly or through views we use the four standard DML statements:

SELECT
DELETE
INSERT
UPDATE

These statements are now universally accepted, as is their functionality, although the degree to which these commands support this functionality varies somewhat between products – compare the functionality of different implementations of UPDATE for example.

The Data Control Statements

Gradually there is becoming increasing agreement on the format and function of these types of commands, which are primarily used to control access to the data. The most commonly found ones will include:

GRANT	to assign privilege
REVOKE	to remove privilege

These three types of statement, the DDL, DML and DCL statements, tend to be relatively stable across all RDBMS, in concept and general format. However, they are accompanied by other statements, where there may be significant differences between different dialects. Typically there will be extensions that are required for the building of specific objects in specific RDBMS products, such as the MODIFY command in Ingres. In general however, these extensions do not contravene the SQL standard because they often reflect different software architectures, and are thus genuinely left to the vendor's discretion. However, where we run into trouble is when different commands are used for the same function – ABORT and ROLLBACK perform the same task on different systems for example, and of greater concern is when some general purpose functions are provided in some products but not in others (the Outer Join function in Oracle for example).

Alongside the more standard DDL, DML and DCL statements you may commonly find commands such as:

COMMIT	to end a transaction
ROLLBACK	to undo a transaction
SAFEPOINT	to create a checkpoint
RELOCATE	to move a table
HELP	to get system/database help
CREATE SYNONYM	to create a preferred object name
SET LOCKMODE	to change default locking
RENAME	to rename a table
CREATE INTEGRITY	to enforce entity integrity rules
CREATE PERMIT	to allocate privilege

For example, Ingres has used in some versions, the CREATE PERMIT statement to restrict user access to data, a problem tackled by the more usual GRANT and REVOKE statements in many other systems, and in deed the syntax preferred in the ANSI standard. COMMIT and ROLLBACK are becoming the standard for transaction management; but Ingres, up to version 5, used BEGIN and END

TRANSACTION whilst implementing ROLLBACK as ABORT, and having a facility for ABORT to defined SAFEPOINTS within transactions. All these features are purely original within the Ingres product.

The significance of the differences in SQL should not be underestimated especially when some of the products have been extended well past the capabilities of others. Gradually, and as there is greater awareness in the benefits of a standard version of SQL, vendors are starting to implement the language with the same commands, but all dialects will still, I feel sure, carry their own extensions. As already mentioned it is very disconcerting to learn that certain facilities in one variety of SQL may not be implemented in another's, and are also not likely to be included in the latest SQL standard. People must make their own mind up as to the content and significance of the SQL standard, and as to the pros and cons of using some of the extensions provided. To illustrate this point some of these extensions are described later.

Returning to the subject of this section, which is a debate on the ease of use of SQL, we have so far isolated one positive advantage in that SQL has only a small number of statements to become familiar with. It is also true to say that many of the statements, particularly the DDL and even more so, the DCL commands, are used relatively infrequently, and mainly by a subset of users – the DBA for example. In general, the application programmer will need to become familiar with the DML statements, and also those addressing transaction management and locking, whilst the terminal user in an SQL session will almost always be restricted to DML statements.

Having noted therefore a certain potential for considering SQL to be 'easy', I am concerned that the overall feeling is that the language is itself an end-user tool to be used for *ad hoc* queries, and it is in this context that the description 'easy to use' is being levelled. Certainly non-DP people can make good and productive use of interactive SQL, and it is true that to master a simple query such as:

SELECT * FROM TABLENAME;

is well within the capabilities of everyone (even though the user will still need to understand the data model to be able to usefully select a table to query upon). If this SELECT is done through a previously defined view, some of the complexities of both SQL and the data model can be hidden from the user to make things even easier. However, reality dictates that to retrieve meaningful data in an *ad hoc* mode will invariably require the use of more complex SQL, coupled with a detailed knowledge of table contents and inter-relationships.

To illustrate the point, let's examine the fundamental structure of the SELECT statement.

SELECT column names
FROM table names
WHERE conditions
ORDER BY sequence of columns;

100

For example:

```
SELECT ENAME, SAL, TUB
FROM EMP
WHERE DEPTNO > 10
ORDER BY DEPTNO;
```

I think at this level the language is accessible to most 'computer aware' professionals, but let us compare this simple example with the syntax of a specific SELECT statement.

```
SELECT [ALL|DISTINCT] {[table.]*|expr[alias],expr[alias],..}
FROM table [alias],table [alias],...
[WHERE condition]
[CONNECT BY condition [START WITH condition]]
[GROUP BY expr,expr,...][HAVING condition]
[{UNION|INTERSECT|MINUS} SELECT...]
[ORDER BY {expr|posn}[ASC|DES],{expr|posn}
[ASC|DESC],...
[FOR UPDATE OF column,column,...[NOWAIT]];
```

We should note here that the [SELECT] in this example shows the subtleness of SQL with its ability to nest SELECTS down to many levels. This gives tremendous power and complexity way beyond the capabilities, but probably not the requirements, of most *ad hoc* users.

To summarise this section therefore, the standardisation on SQL as the prime RDBMS language is a tremendous asset to all concerned. SQL is a concise and very powerful non-procedural language which, in its simplest form, can be easy to use; whilst in its complex form, is capable of all the requirements necessary to drive large scale database systems. Most RDBMSs do provide general purpose tools for end-user queries, but interactive SQL should not in my opinion be thought of as one of them. At an interactive terminal, SQL is usefully used for bench-marking and data administration work. I would also suggest that success is certainly possible in the production world, but probably in the hands of the MIS professional rather than the so called 'end-user'.

The Portability Issue

SQL was adopted in 1986 by the American National Standards Institute (ANSI) as the official standard language for RDBMS, and certainly all vendors of nearly all DBMSs have sought in the recent past to provide an SQL/Relational interface to their products. We should be aware though that SQL was not part of the overall relational design and was in fact an 'add on' feature.

Of course, just as a database can pretend to be relational by supporting tables and columns at the logical level to the user, so the DBMS can pretend to be an SQL database, simply by translating user-provided SQL into another language to perform the database accesses, and in fact this is exactly how the Ingres product initially supported SQL. However this need not concern us unduly, as the portability issue is really about database structures and data access through SQL on different products.

The term portability, as used by most people when questioned about their perceived advantage of SQL, refers to the ability to transport SQL programs and data structures between different vendor's database systems. We might therefore expect SQL programs, that currently define data structures and manipulate data in a Sybase database, to convert with little or no modification to run against DB2. If this was a reality we would gain the ability of changing DBMSs whilst protecting investment in applications code; a state of affairs which would be highly desirable indeed.

Whilst there are great efforts being made to devise an SQL standard language, which would help in allowing the achievement of this goal, there are three real problems as the situation stands at present, which refer back to points already made previously. These are that:

❑ Different vendors have achieved the same functionality in different ways.

❑ Some vendors have extended the SQL product way beyond that of the current standard.

❑ Different databases have fundamentally different architectures, security features and auditing facilities, which make it very difficult to come up with a standard set of commands.

It is true to say therefore that there are many varieties of SQL (one per RDBMS product in reality), and whilst they are all very similar in scope and functionality, there are sufficient differences to make it unrealistic to expect a specific version to work with a non-native RDBMS, without some sort of modification. However, having pointed this out, it is very reassuring to know that understanding the basic constraints will allow successful integration of many different vendor offerings. A command such as: SELECT, UPDATE, INSERT or DELETE is likely, in its simple form, to be fairly standard between products, but this is not true when one tries to nest these commands using sub-selects or to use functions, or even formatting commands. There are indeed many detailed differences between products, especially when dealing with null values, functions and the handling of column heading, date and time. At the DDL level the case starts to get truly hopeless. Whilst the underlying CREATE TABLE, VIEW and INDEX statements do appear to share some symmetry, I have illustrated below some different CREATE TABLE commands just to illustrate how different they can be.

The **Oracle** statement includes the following syntax:

```
CREATE TABLE tablename
        (column spec [NULL | NOT NULL],....)
        [SPACE space-definition [PCTFREE n] |
        CLUSTER clustername (column,.....)];
```

Here the SPACE extension allows the table to be created with some predefined location and storage characteristics, and the CLUSTER extension is a provision for ensuring that rows from different tables can be located together on disk.

The **Ingres** statement uses a different syntax, thus:

```
CREATE TABLE
        [location name:]tablename
        (column spec .......)
        [WITH JOURNALLING];
```

In this example, prefixing a table name with a location enables the placing of tables on specific hardware, and the JOURNALLING option is used to switch After Image Journalling on for a specific table.

It is very difficult, therefore, to draw firm conclusions about the portability issue concerning SQL. Certainly when you know one dialect of the language you can easily assimilate others, although it can get a trifle annoying at times as you run into inconsistencies at even the most basic levels. The issue of running the same code successfully against different database products is less obvious. Certainly the principles are, the same and simple code will not require wholesale changes. For large scale applications however, the task can be expected to be of some dimension and probably well worth leaving alone, to be handled rather by specialised Gateway software which is described elsewhere.

Some Important SQL Extensions

Before moving on, I'd like to illustrate a couple of the more well known SQL extensions, to give a feel for the nature of some of the differences in functionality to be found between some versions of SQL. The ones I have chosen have important implications because they represent common areas of requirement, and are clumsy to handle without the specifically designed extensions.

Hierarchical Data Structure Support

This facility, and I believe currently it's only supported in the Oracle product, allows hierarchical reports to be produced from flat two-dimensional relational tables. In order to demonstrate this rather unique feature let's examine the following query:

```
SELECT LEVEL,ENAME,EMPNO,JOB,DEPTNO,MGR
FROM EMP
CONNECT BY PRIOR EMPNO = MGR
START WITH DNAME = 'JONES'
ORDER BY DEPTNO;
```

This example uses a self-referencing table in which the MGR and EMPNO values come from the same domain and can be usefully related to find out the name of any employee's manager. This relationship is defined in the query with the CONNECT BY extension, and so the SQL can be interpreted as 'give me the rows from the table, presented in an order reflecting the relationship of employees to managers, so that I see a management hierarchy starting at the top with 'JONES'. The resulting report might look like this:

LEVEL	ENAME	EMPNO	JOB	DEPTNO	MGR
1	JONES	834	President	5	Null
2	BROWN	782	Mgr	5	834
3	MILLER	934	Clerk	5	782
2	SMITH	566	Mgr	10	834
3	PAGE	902	Analyst	10	566
4	GREEN	369	Clerk	10	902
3	SWIFT	788	Analyst	10	566
4	ADAMS	876	Clerk	10	788
2	PATE	698	Mgr	20	834
3	BOYD	844	Salesman	20	698
3	BOYCE	900	Clerk	20	698
3	LINCOLN	654	Salesman	30	698
3	COOK	521	Salesman	30	698

Diagrammatically the output may look like this:

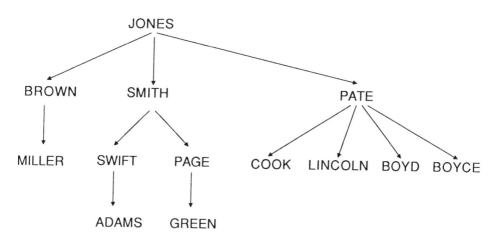

On the face of it, this extension appears to be very powerful indeed although it is certainly relevant if a certain underlying structure is inherent in the data itself.

Outer Joins

Again it's easiest to explain the concept of an Outer Join with reference to an example. Let's imagine a simple set of tables designed to help in the recording of examination results:

PEOPLE

Name	Age	Sex
Jon	16	m
Ted	18	m
Bill	16	m
Joe	15	m

EXAMS

Title	Date
Biology	26/7/88
Chemistry	26/7/88
Maths	26/9/88

RESULTS

Name	Title	Grade
Bill	Biology	3
Joe	Biology	2
Joe	Chemistry	4
Jon	Biology	3

Now suppose we wanted to retrieve a list of all people, and their grades in exams if they have taken any, in order to compile a report as follows:

Name	Title	Grade	Age
Jon	Biology	3	16
Ted			18
Bill	Biology	3	16
Joe	Chemistry	4	15
Joe	Biology	2	15

You will see that a straight join across the PEOPLE and RESULTS tables will not select the row identified by Ted because Ted has no row in the Results table. Our requirement is for an operation called an Outer Join.

Now there are various ways of achieving this result. In some varieties of SQL there is a rather convenient Outer Join operator which makes the job somewhat trivial.

```
SELECT A.NAME,B.TITLE,B.GRADE,A.AGE
FROM PEOPLE A,RESULTS B
WHERE A.NAME = B.NAME(+);
```

However you're unlikely to ever see this function in the standard SQL, so most people will have to solve this problem using one of two fairly unattractive methods. It can be done by aggregating the results of two queries with a UNION, or if this is an unsupported function, then the same can be achieved using a temporary table. It is actually possible to do the whole job with the NOT EXISTS operator – you may like to try this for yourself, if you have access to a version of SQL that supports this construct.

Correlated Queries

As already mentioned, a great deal of the power of SQL originates from the ability to construct complex statements with the use of sub-queries being connected together with operators such as < > = NOT IN and ANY.

A great deal of care is needed when comparing different dialects of the language, because the support of the sub-query construct and the functional power of it, varies enormously from version to version. Currently there are some infuriating gaps in some implementations, and the next example of correlated queries is in general very poorly supported.

A simple example of the use of a sub-query is described below:

```
SELECT ENAME,JOB FROM EMP
WHERE DEPTNO = 10
AND JOB IN
    (SELECT JOB FROM EMP WHERE DEPTNO = 30);
```

This query is evaluated in two stages: firstly, the subquery is executed, and a list of all jobs held by employees in department 30 is created. Secondly, the details of people from department 10 are retrieved, where their jobs match any in the list produced by the sub-query. In short, the sub-query is evaluated once and its results are compared to each row retrieved by the main query.

However suppose we wish to find employees who earn more than the average salary in their own department. Again we need a two-phased approach, but there is a subtle difference between this and our last example. In this query, for every row retrieved by the main query, we need to perform the sub-query to calculate the average salary in his department, so the processing is much more driven by the main query than in the above example.

```
SELECT * FROM EMP X
WHERE SAL >
    (SELECT AVG(SAL)
    FROM EMP
    WHERE X.DEPTNO = DEPTNO);
```

The correlation above, is activated in Oracle SQL by the use of the table alias (X in this case) but as this is not a standard feature of SQL as yet, this should not be considered universal. The effect of the X is that it enforces row level referencing, so that X.DEPTNO refers back to the single row being selected from the main query. In other words, for every row selected in the main query, the sub-query is executed with the single value of the employee's DEPTNO used as the X.DEPTNO.

The point of this example is two fold: firstly correlated queries are very much an SQL extension and a very powerful one at that; secondly they are supported in very few dialects of the language. Anyone porting Oracle SQL containing either this construct or the outer join, can expect to find themselves with a lot of work indeed!

Some other Anomalies in SQL

Certainly whilst SQL has been accepted for the time being as the standard relational database access language, it has its critics. Restrictions caused by its set-driven orientation can often be overcome by embedding it in a more traditional row-at-a-time language such as COBOL but SQL falls down on other rather esoteric points some of which are described below, more out of interest than of real criticism.

Entity Integrity

Standard SQL currently employs two restricting methods of ensuring some degree of entity integrity.

The NOT NULL operator ensures that a row, when inserted into a table, has a value associated with every column to which the NOT NULL prefix was supplied in that table's CREATE TABLE statement.

The UNIQUE extension within the CREATE INDEX command ensures that every entry in a table has a unique value for the data in the column or columns over which the unique index was built. As extensions to this idea, many dialects have other types of constraints, which are described elsewhere in this book.

What we have therefore, is a situation where a very important relational concept has been left for different vendors to implement in their own way, to what ever degree of completeness they think fit. The rules of a primary key on a relation are clear, in as much as the data values must be unique and null values are not allowed, so why not have an extension to the CREATE TABLE command that simply enforces these simple rules by defining a primary key for every relation?

```
CREATE TABLE tablename (
PRODNO INTEGER,
DESC CHAR(10))
PRIMARY-KEY PRODNO;
```

SQL and Duplicate Rows

It is a clearly stated rule of relational theory that every row in a relation must have a unique identifier, and what this clearly translates to, for the benefit of the lay reader, is that a relation must contain no duplicate rows. This is so clear-cut and easy to understand that it surprises me that the vast majority of RDBMSs do allow such anomalies, there being very few – Teradata DBC/SQL being of noteworthy exception – that actually support the requirement of no duplicity in rows. Undoubtedly there is a common perception that duplicate rows must be allowed if statistical functions such as *sum* and *average* are to give correct results. This thought should be dismissed at an early stage because it is based on a clear relational untruth. What is the point of having entirely duplicate rows? A computer need be told something only once and exaggerating the point does not have any great significance to any processor that I know of!

There are other reasons why duplicate rows should not be allowed and really the ANSI standard should outlaw this dangerous state of affairs. Let's illustrate the point with some examples:

Let's presume that our RDBMS allows duplicate rows and provides the SQL DISTINCT operator to remove them from the result set when required.

```
R(A     B     C)      S(D E)
a1      1     c1       d1  1
a2      1     c1       d2  1
a3      1     c2       d3  2
a4      2     c2
a5      2     c1
```

Now, on the above tables suppose we perform a projection R(B,C) first allowing duplicates, and then take this result set and perform an equi-join to S(E) this time discarding duplicates. You may like to satisfy yourself that you will end up with six rows with no duplicates.

Projection (with dups)   Equi Join (no dups)

B	C
1	C1
1	C2
2	C2
2	C1

B	C
1	C1
1	C1
1	C2
1	C2
2	C2
2	C1

= 6 result rows

Now let's reverse the exercise and perform the equi-join first, not allowing duplicates in the result, followed by the projection allowing duplicates. If you've done your sums correctly you should now have eight rows.

Equi Join (no dups)   Projection (with dups)

A	C	D	B/E
A1	C1	D1	1
A1	C1	D2	1
A2	C1	D1	1
A2	C1	D2	1
A3	C2	D1	1
A3	C2	D2	1
A4	C2	D3	2
A5	C1	D3	2

B/E	C
1	C1
1	C1
1	C1
1	C1
1	C2
1	C2
2	C2
2	C1

This illustrates the alarming results that can occur when a confused policy on duplicate rows is allowed.

Before leaving this area let's continue to unearth some further 'features' or certain implementations of SQL. If an RDBMS allows duplicate rows we have already seen that the order in which queries are executed can effect the results. Unfortunately the structure of the query itself can also confuse the issue.

EMP   WAREHOUSE

EMPNO	ECITY
E1	LONDON
E2	NEW YORK
E3	BOSTON

WNAME	WCITY
W1	LONDON
W1	LONDON
W2	LIVERPOOL
W3	BOSTON
W4	TOKYO

Supposing we wished to ask: 'give me all the employees and the city in which they work, where that city has a warehouse'.

Such a query can be fulfilled by either a nested query with an IN operator:

```
SELECT EMPNO, ECITY FROM EMP
WHERE ECITY IN
(SELECT WCITY FROM WAREHOUSE)
```

or a simple equi-join:

```
SELECT EMPNO,ECITY FROM EMP,WAREHOUSE
WHERE EMP.ECITY = WAREHOUSE.WCITY
```

You will find, however, that the results returned may be different if duplicate rows are supported. From the first query we will retrieve:

EMPNO	ECITY
E1	LONDON
E3	BOSTON

From the second we will get:

EMPNO	ECITY
E1	LONDON
E1	LONDON
E3	BOSTON

Upserts

It's likely that not many people will have come across the Upsert, so I include it here as a matter of interest.

Some versions of SQL allow this type of construct in the UPDATE command:

TAB1

COL1	COL2
A	1
B	5
X	2

TAB2

COL1	COL2
X	3
A	6

```
UPDATE TAB1 SET COL2 = TAB2.COL2
WHERE TAB1.COL1 = TAB2.COL1;
```

If this was executed on the example tables we might expect that Tab1 would end up as:

110

TAB1

COL1	COL2
A	6
B	5
X	3

If by accident however, the WHERE clause is left out we find, in some products, that our update actually inserts rows giving a result in our example of:

TAB1

COL1	COL2
A	3
B	6
X	3
A	6
B	3
X	6

What I've tried to do in this chapter is to focus the mind on some of the more interesting aspects of SQL. There are plenty of others out there to be found but I do not wish to labour the point. SQL is a powerful language and we are right in using it. It is in its infancy, however, and certainly does not have the stability of such languages as COBOL or FORTRAN, but its existence could possibly have even greater long-term significance than either of these. If the use of SQL focuses minds on the benefits of a standard language, then we can forgive the odd quirks I have outlined here as being merely growing pains.

Summary

1) Two of the major advantages of using SQL are professed to be ease of use and portability. Certainly there are aspects of the language that assist in both of these areas, but there is a long way to go yet.

2) Beware of some of the more potent SQL extensions. It's not always easy to tell which bits are vendor specific and it will be very easy to write non-portable code and thus waste potential benefit.

3) Different dialects of SQL can arrive at their result sets in different ways even, if

they were originally presented with the same SQL command. You may well find that the result set returned from one version will not be the one that you expected.

4) Be also aware that it often seems possible to achieve the same result set in different ways. You can often arrive at the expected result by luck, but that luck may desert you one day.

References

C.J. Date, A Guide to the SQL Standard *Addison Wesley* 1987

ANSI SQL2 Standard Document ANSI X3H2-89-151

R.F. van der Lans ,The SQL Standard A Complete Reference *Prentice Hall*

J. Harvey Trimble, D. Chappell, A Visual Introduction to SQL *John Wiley & Sons* 1989

Emerson, Darnousky, Bowman, The Practical SQL Handbook *Addison-Wesley*

9

Indexing

Imagine for a moment you're anxious to know the meaning of the word 'perplex' and it just so happens that you're in the vicinity of a public library. You may have never been in this library before, but as you walk in there are some obvious pointers to aid your cause. First you may see a notice directing you to reference books, and there you may find other helpful indications as to where you may find information about such subjects as Art, Model Making, Computers and lo and behold! Dictionaries. Well, it's all easy so far – in two minutes you've managed to discount ten thousand books as not being helpful to you and now there are just five to select from. Well, you don't know much about dictionaries so you pick the first one and open it somewhere in the middle. Now it's fortunate that all the entries in the dictionary are in alphabetical order and each page holds at the top, the first and last entry on that page because from here in it takes just three or four page selections and a final scan down the page to locate 'perplex':

''greatly puzzle or disconcert, complicate or confuse''

This little example points out how it's possible to extract small points of detail from an overwhelming amount. It's these same ideas, implemented largely with indexes, that allow the same direct and quick access to data in RDBMSs.

What is an Index?

Using the above example, it should be clear that within a library system, very small amounts of data can be extracted from enormous quantities fairly quickly. This is due mainly to three features:

❏ The library has signs to direct activity usefully.

❏ People generally understand the principle of how the library functions.

❑ Books have some sort of logical organisation that is again well understood by most.

If no such structure was present, it would be a daunting task indeed to look through the titles of all the ten thousand or so books present in the library, in search of a dictionary. Even this time would be short compared to that required in examining every single entry in that dictionary until the word 'perplexed' was found, especially if the entries were in random order. On average, if there were ten thousand books and five were dictionaries, we would have looked at two thousand books before locating a dictionary, and then with ten thousand entries in the book, we would need to have examined five thousand of them before finding our word.

The above example should make it quite clear that when we are faced with the prospect of accessing rows from our database tables, which we know by definition are held in random order, we will need some help. Without any pointers (indexes) and with no inherent organisation in the rows to find any particular item, we are likely to be faced with reading every row in the table. This is termed a 'full table scan' and below is a simple example:

SELECT EMPLOYEENAME FROM EMP WHERE EMPNO = 1000;

On average this query will need to search half the table even with the benefit of knowing that EMPNOs are unique.

The query:

SELECT EMPLOYEENAME FROM EMP WHERE EMPNO LIKE '1%';

will certainly have to search the whole table to ensure that it retrieves all qualifying rows.

So what is the answer in the relational database world?

Just as in the library we employ both signs and some inherent organisation to optimise access to what could otherwise be random data, in the relational database world, where quick access to data is required, the technique of indexing is used.

An index is, in broad terms, a separate database structure which is used to make access into a specific table quicker. The creation and deletion of indexes is dynamic in SQL, being actioned with variations on the familiar CREATE and DROP commands, and such structures can be built on any column or combinations of columns in a single table, and similarly dropped. Some versions of SQL allow a MODIFY command that I will discuss later, and Oracle includes a VALIDATE statement allowing some degree of maintenance work to be performed on indexes; however, these are by no means universal.

There are two major types of indexing in common use at the moment and by describing each, the principles of index usage should become clear.

The Btree Index

By far the most common type of structure, the Btree is found in widespread use in many relational systems. In many ways, its performance is a compromise between methods that give very fast single row access, and those types that optimise range search activity such as:

SELECT * FROM TABLE WHERE COLUMN LIKE 'sm%';

Let's use the following table as an example:

EMPNAME	AGE
BLACK	23
BROWN	25
BOYCE	61
BOYD	45
CLARK	34
GREEN	53
JONES	54
LINCOLN	43
NEAL	54
PIMM	43
RILEY	34
RUSH	34
SMEDLEY	44
SMITH	33

We might decide that because we almost always access this table by EMPNAME it would be worth building a Btree index on that specific column.

A typical SQL statement to execute this might be:

CREATE INDEX NAMEIND ON EMP(EMPNAME);

The command, which can be executed interactively, will build an index structure with the logical representation shown in Figure 9.1 on the next page:

Now how does this index help? Suppose we enter the following query:

SELECT * FROM EMP WHERE EMPNAME = 'CLARK';

There are two ways in which this query can be executed: firstly, every record can be read, and all rows where EMPNAME = 'CLARK' returned as the result set – this is termed a full table scan. Secondly the index can be used in the following way:

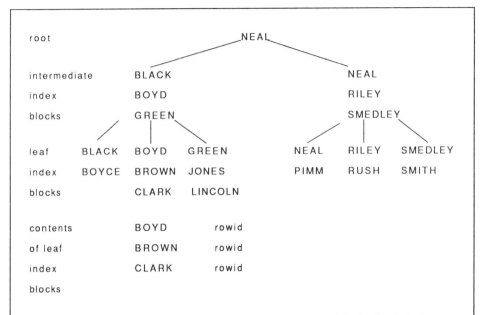

Figure 9.1 The Btree Index (I have stolen the idea of rowid from Oracle – it is simply a logical row address in the actual database.)

The root value is read, and because NEAL is greater than CLARK, the leftmost intermediate index block is read.

CLARK is greater than BOYD, but less than GREEN, so the leaf index block that is pointed to by the BOYD entry is read.

This leaf block is scanned to find the CLARK entry, and its rowid is used to locate the actual record.

When expressed like this, you may be forgiven for thinking that the use of the index must be slow. However consider the situation where you are accessing a single row from a table which spans one hundred thousand disk blocks. A full table scan in this situation would require one hundred thousand expensive I/O operations and, if the data was on a single disk capable of the industry standard 30 I/Os per second, this could take some time. However, using the index would probably need no more than four such I/Os – the root, intermediate and leaf blocks of the index followed by direct access to the data-block. It's also likely that some of this index information, if accessed regularly, will be resident in memory thus cutting down on I/O even more.

It can be seen from this example of the Btree, that every single row in the data table has a corresponding entry at the leaf level which holds that row's address, and it is this characteristic that gives the Btree the qualification of being a 'Dense' index organisation. Because all the row addresses are held in the index in key order then any serial access to the index will result in the data itself being returned in key order.

This last feature can be of considerable benefit, but does mean that whenever a row is inserted into or deleted from a table carrying a Btree index then the index has to be modified to reflect this change. This will obviously constitute an overhead. However there is a good side to even this because, as there is no need for the data row to be in any particular place on the disk, this type of organisation suffers from no overflow problems.

Because this Btree structure is so commonplace, it is worth simply listing some of the more important advantages and disadvantages.

Advantages of Btree indexes:

1) Because there is no overflow problem inherent with this type of organisation it is good for dynamic tables – those that suffer a great deal of insert/update/delete activity.

2) Because it is to a large extent self-maintaining, it is good in supporting 24-hour operation.

3) As data is retrieved via the index it is always presented in order.

4) 'Get next' queries are efficient because of the inherent ordering of rows within the index blocks.

5) Btree indexes are good for very large tables because they will need minimal reorganisation.

6) There is predictable access time for any retrieval (of the same number of rows of course) because the Btree structure keeps itself balanced, so that there is always the same number of index levels for every retrieval. Bear in mind of course, that the number of index levels does increase both with the number of records and the length of the key value.

Because the rows are in order, this type of index can service range type enquiries, of the type below, efficiently.

SELECT ... WHERE COL BETWEEN X AND Y;

Disadvantages of Btree indexes:

1) For static tables, there are better organisations that require fewer I/Os. ISAM indexes are preferable to Btree in this type of environment.

2) Btree is not really appropriate for very small tables because index look-up becomes a significant part of the overall access time.

3) The index can use considerable disk space, especially in products which allow different users to create separate indexes on the same table/column combinations.

4) Because the indexes themselves are subject to modification when rows are

updated, deleted or inserted, they are also subject to locking which can inhibit concurrency.

So to conclude this section on Btree indexes, it is worth stressing that this structure is by far and away the most popular, and perhaps versatile, of index structures supported in the world of the RDBMS today. Whilst not fully optimised for certain activity, it is seen as the best single compromise in satisfying all the different access methods likely to be required in normal day-to-day operation.

The ISAM Index

The Indexed Sequential Access Method (ISAM) is nothing new in the world of file organisations, but it is rare to find it as an option in a relational database. Certainly Oracle does not support it, whilst Ingres ranks it as an important access method for some of the reasons outlined below.

Unlike the Btree, the ISAM index is not 'dense', and by this I mean that there is not a level of index entries on a one-to-one basis with the data rows, but rather pointers pointing to whole blocks of them – this is known as a 'sparse' index. The following figure illustrates its functioning.

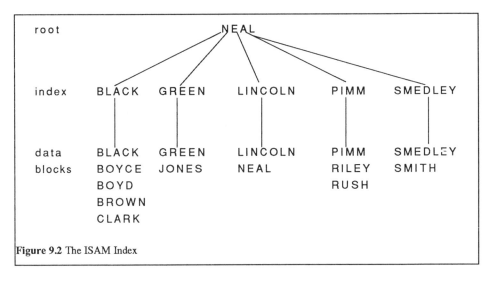

Figure 9.2 The ISAM Index

You may notice from the above that there are some fundamental differences between ISAM and Btree. If for example, we are again looking for CLARK we are, just as before, diverted down the left side of our index as CLARK is less than NEAL. Now however, the situation changes. At the next level of index we can ascertain that CLARK is greater than BLACK, but less than GREEN, so the data row for CLARK is to be found in the block that is pointed to by the BLACK index entry. The next action therefore is to retrieve this data block and scan it for the CLARK record. Now if we are unlucky we'll hit on a problem that has been mentioned before and that does not effect the Btree structure. If you examine the ISAM index carefully you will notice that for it to work, the data rows must be kept in order in the logical sense because the index itself is static. This means that one of our data blocks contains rows valued between PIMM and RUSH, and this must always remain true until the next time the index itself is dropped and rebuild (or modified in the case of Ingres).

The problem is, therefore, that if many records with key values between PIMM and RUSH are inserted into this table, the block pointed to by the index and physically holding these rows, will quickly become full. Under these circumstances the data is said to overflow, and the rows that no longer fit will be moved to another 'overflow block', with a tag left in the original block saying where they can be found. Thus even when we have found the data block where the row for CLARK should be, we cannot guarantee its presence, and we might have to search overflow blocks to locate it.

There is another problem implicit in this because generally, overflow blocks are just serial lists of all rows which have overflowed for a specific block. Each overflow block, and there may be many of them over a period of time, is simply chained to the next. In the case of a major overflow, several overflow blocks may need to be scanned to locate a row, and this can have serious consequences on performance, especially when coupled with potential locking problems which are explained elsewhere.

So what is the significance of the ISAM organisation?

Advantages of ISAM indexes:

1) Because the whole structure is ordered to a large extent, partial (LIKE ty%) and range (BETWEEN 12 and 18) based retrievals can often benefit from the use of this type of index.

2) ISAM is good for static tables because there are usually fewer index levels than Btree.

3) Because the Index is never updated, there are never any locking contention problems within the index itself – this can occur in Btree indexes, especially when they get to the point of 'splitting' to create another level.

4) In general there are fewer disk I/Os required to access data, provided there is no overflow.

5) Again if little overflow is evident, then data tends to be clustered. This means that a single block retrieval often brings back rows with similar key values and of relevance to the initiating query.

Disadvantages of ISAM indexes:

1) ISAM is still not as quick as some (hash organisation, dealt with later, is quicker).

2) Overflow can be a real problem in highly volatile tables.

3) The sparse index means that the lowest level of index has only the highest key for a specific data page, and therefore the block (or more usually a block header), must be searched to locate specific rows in a block.

In a nutshell therefore, these are the two types of indexing generally available. As I have already said, indexes can be either created on one single, or several groups, of columns within single tables, and generally the ability to create them should be a privilege under the control of the DBA. Indexes usually take up significant disk space, and although generally of significant benefit in the case of data retrieval, they can slow down insert/update and delete operation because of overhead in maintaining the index, and in ISAM of ensuring the logical organisation of the data rows. The presence of an index does not mean that the RDBMS will always use it, a reality of life discussed later; and it is also true that it is not generally possible to pick and choose which index will be used under which conditions. It follows, therefore, that the administration of indexes should be done centrally, with great care, and should be a major consideration in the physical design stage of a project due to its application dependence.

Before leaving these types of access mechanisms and moving on to an explanation of hashing, it is worth listing some of the other functions that may be required within the context of manipulating indexes.

Row Uniqueness

A very important function of an index is its ability to reject rows with non-unique values in the column or column combinations defined as the unique index. A unique index built on the primary key of a relation is a very powerful tool to help in ensuring data integrity and being under central control adds value to this power. Remember though that row uniqueness is a logical consideration, and to enforce it outside the scope of an application is likely to be dangerous. Index creation and deletion is a dynamic activity, and the uniqueness of an index can be lost by dropping an index specified as unique and recreating it as non-unique.

Compression

As the indexes themselves are tables of some significance some products allow compression techniques to cut down the disk space used by the index itself. Here you will need to balance disk space savings, which will enable not only resource saving but the bringing back of more index information per I/O, with the CPU power needed in both compression and decompression. In fact most RDBMSs support compression of data rows as well as indexes, and there are a variety of ways in which it can be done including:

❑ Removing trailing spaces

❑ Replacing common characters with smaller bit patterns

❑ Replacing sequences of the same character with a single occurrence of that character, and a count of how many times it is present consecutively

❑ Forward and backward compression where an entry is formulated from those before it or after it – a facility that demands that the entries are sorted.

Fillfactors

When a Btree index block gets full, it splits its contents into further blocks. To avoid this it is prudent to never fill the blocks to 100% on initial creation and thus in Oracle, a PCTFREE option allows you to leave say, 20% of each block free, whilst conversely an 80% FILLFACTOR in Ingres accomplishes the same thing (80 is the Btree default anyway). Such facilities can be of significance.

Modify

Because Ingres, for example, supports more than one type of index it has a MODIFY command which has two main functions:

❑ To reorganise data/indexes

❑ To change an index structure

Therefore if a table called EMP had an ISAM index on EMPNAME and we decided that, because a lot of update activity had occurred, it was time to reorganise it to recover overflow pages, we would issue the command:

    MODIFY EMP TO ISAM ON EMPNAME;

If we then decided that perhaps it would be better as a Btree index anyway, we might say:

    MODIFY EMP TO BTREE ON EMPNAME;

Although certainly not common, there are two further types of organisation that are worthy of some attention, because they are implemented in two major RDBMS products, namely hash organisation available in Ingres and Teradata and bit-mapped indexes available also as a feature of the Teradata product.

Hash Organisation

Another somewhat old-fashioned, but highly relevant file organisation that is implemented in some RDBMSs is that of the hash organisation. In short hashing involves the placement of each row of a table at a logical address that is computed by passing that row's prime index value through what is commonly termed a 'hashing algorithm'. Thus when a row (say CLARK) is first inserted into a table its key value is converted to a logical address and it is at this location that the record is stored.

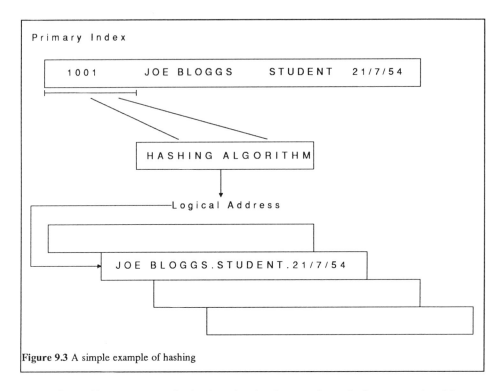

Figure 9.3 A simple example of hashing

To retrieve this same record, the key is simply put through the same algorithm to reveal the same address, and hence the row is directly retrievable. As in the ISAM organisation, overflow can be a problem because rows with the same key value will hash always to the same address. It is also possible that rows with completely different key values will end up as 'hash synonyms', hashing to the same block thus causing potential overflow problems. To summarise the advantages and disadvantages of this approach:

Advantages of hashing:

1) Exact key matches are extremely quick.

2) Hashing is very good for long keys, or those with multiple columns, provided the complete key value is provided for the query.

3) This organisation usually allows for the allocation of disk space so a good deal of disk management is possible.

4) No disk space is used by this indexing method.

Disadvantages of hashing:

1) It becomes difficult to predict overflow because the workings of the hashing algorithm will not be visible to the DBA.

2) No sorting of data occurs either physically or logically so sequential access is poor.

3) This organisation usually takes a lot of disk space to ensure that no overflow occurs – there is a plus side to this though: no space is wasted on index structures because they simply don't exist.

To sum up hashing it's true to say that not many products support this type of structure, and it is likely, I feel, to become entirely redundant in most software RDBMSs. An interesting contradiction to this is the Teradata DBC, which distributes all its data to multiple disk drives, based purely on hashing the columns that will comprise the primary access path to the data, and this point needs to be stressed. In a hashing organisation, the key that is hashed should be the one that is used most to retrieve the data (or join it to other tables) and this will often not be the primary key that I have previously defined within the scope of logical data design.

Bit-mapped Indexing

Probably the rarest type of indexing to be found in the relational world is called bit-mapped indexing. Again it is not a new idea, and finds favour when data suffers from many duplicate values and has several non-unique indexes.

Take the following table as an example, and assume that there is a non-unique indent built on each of the columns, C1, C2 and C3:

C1	C2	C3	ROWID
1	3	6	1
1	5	6	4
1	3	7	3
4	3	6	2

Suppose we ask a query:

```
SELECT * FROM TABLE
WHERE     C1 = 1
AND       C2 = 3
AND       C3 = 7;
```

Access by bit-mapping requires the following activities to be performed by the RDBMS:

❑ Bit-maps will be produced for the three indexes in the following way:

C1 = 1

ROWID	1	2	3	4
Does row qualify?	1	0	1	1

C2 = 3

ROWID	1	2	3	4
Does row qualify?	1	1	1	0

C3 = 7

ROWID	1	2	3	4
Does row qualify?	0	0	1	0

❏ These bit-maps (the 'does row qualify' bit!) are then combined using the AND operator, to produce a final access bit-map:

1	0	1	1
1	1	1	0
0	0	1	0
0	0	1	0

❏ This final map when compared to our list of ROWIDs should reveal that only ROWID 3 satisfies this query:

Bit-map	0	0	1	0
ROWID	1	2	3	4

We therefore have a very concise and powerful way of resolving some fairly complex queries, but we should remember that very few – I know of only the Teradata system at present, support this type of access. It generally finds favour with queries that have many WHERE predicates, none of which are very restrictive but when evaluated together become quite specific. To conclude this section on index types, the table on the following page attempts to show under what different circumstances different types of index should be considered.

Table 9.1 Index Usage Summary

	HEAP	HASH	ISAM	BTREE
Bulk loading data to table	1			
Removing duplicates		1	1	1
Exact match		1	1	2
Range/pattern match			2	1
Sequential search	3		2	1
Partial key			2	1
Access to sorted data			2	1
Joins on large tables	2			1
Index grows as table grows				1
Very small table	1			
Very large table	1	1		

HEAP = no indexes at all, a random collection of rows
number = ranking of appropriateness
blank = inappropriate

Summary

1) The provision and maintenance of relevant indexes in a relational database is absolutely fundamental to its performance, and unfortunately can have consequences on the integrity of data within the database.

2) Indexes are build to help physical access to data and their appropriateness does not follow obviously from the task of logical database design.

3) Indexes are also build to preserve data integrity and in these cases the requirement should be defined within the scope of logical data design.

4) The provision of indexes is something done by people; whether the indexes are used or not, is largely a decision made by the RDBMS itself and that is the subject of the next chapter.

10

Optimisation

We have already dealt with the subject of indexes and so we are in a good position to bring up the subject of query optimisation. As previously mentioned, it is not the user's job to tell the RDBMS how to access data but rather to design a database sensibly to provide, in the form of indexes, efficient access paths for the RDBMS to use, and then hope that it uses them. When the RDBMS makes its decision on your behalf, concerning how it will retrieve data for you, it uses both the information that has been provided for it by you, or more likely the DBA, and its own 'intelligence'. This decision is made by code commonly called the optimiser. This chapter explains the role of the optimiser, and some of the ways in which it goes about its business.

The Role of the Optimiser

Let's start this discussion on Query Optimisation by using the following query as an example:

SELECT * FROM STAFF

WHERE DEPTNO = 100

AND GRADE = 'CLERK';

When such a query is entered by a user it goes through a few stages before execution.

Firstly, the query will be checked for any syntax errors, for example SELECT spelt SELEKT. Any such errors will halt further processing of the query, causing an error message to be returned to the user, with some type of diagnostic advice on how to put the statement right.

Following this, the semantics of the statement will be checked by the parser, and object names (tables and columns) may be translated into more manageable identifiers. The dictionary will be consulted to check whether this user has sufficient privilege to execute this type of command, and eventually the RDBMS may decide that it is OK to execute this request.

Before converting the statement into executable steps, the system must evaluate the best method of executing the request, and this is the job of the aforementioned optimiser.

So, returning to the example, and presuming there to be an index on both DEPTNO and GRADE, the optimiser must choose the best out of at least four access paths. It may:

❏ Do a full table scan of table STAFF, discounting those rows not matching the requirement

❏ Use an index on DEPTNO, thus bringing back a reasonably small result set through, which it will need to check for GRADE = 'CLERK'

❏ Use an index on GRADE thus retrieving several hundred records for checking DEPTNO = 100

❏ Use both indexes and sort/merge the two result sets.

The user who entered this query cannot influence the optimiser directly in its choice on how to execute the query he must sit and hope the optimiser chooses the best method.

As we have just seen, the DBMS has to make certain choices when deciding how to execute a given SQL statement and these different execution methods are often known as Query Execution Plans (QEP). Prior to relational systems, the user not only had to specify what data was required, but also how to get it, and, as you will be aware, a prime objective of the relational model is to allow the DBMS to decide the 'how' bit, thus freeing the user to supply just the 'what' part. So, what sort of information does this optimiser base its decisions on?

The basic information required by the optimiser will be details about the indexes available to satisfy the query, and information about the distribution of data values in the target columns. Both these types of data should be held and maintained in the data dictionary, although it should be mentioned that whilst the former information is kept up to date in the dictionary, the latter data tends to be gathered by running utilities, and thus only represents a picture of the data as it was when the utility was last run.

If no data statistics are available, because the DBA has not been running the statistics gathering utilities, most systems will use preset default values. It is often difficult to find out from the vendors what these defaults are. DB2 for example, at least at present, assumes that the first column of an index will have 25 different values unless it is told differently, and this tendency, to believe by default that data is normally distributed, can cause problems. Ingres assumes that all queries of the nature $X = Y$

are very selective, so tends to use indexes where possible on these types of query, even if in fact, there is only one distinct value of Y in the whole column. If no indexes are available, or the available ones are not suitable, then full table scans are initiated.

In order to explain how query optimisation works, I am going to split the subject into two sections. Below are some examples of optimising single table queries, but the real complexity of the subject is only really seen in JOIN processing, so later I explain how most RDBMSs go about JOINing tables under different circumstances.

Let's firstly use some examples to show how optimisation may occur in single table queries.

Example 1

Suppose we have a table on which a column called SEX has a non-unique index. A query of the type:

```
SELECT * FROM TABLE WHERE SEX = 'M';
```

would likely retrieve about 50% of the rows from the table. The query optimisers in common use today, tend to believe by default that queries, such as the above, are very selective, so the optimiser will decide to use the index. In this example, using an index to retrieve 50% of all rows is very expensive, compared to a full table scan, because to read half of the rows, will probably require the reading of all the data blocks. Under such circumstances there is no reason to read the index which merely constitutes an overhead. Therefore indexes on columns that do not have many distinct values are usually fairly inefficient, and in our SEX example it would be unwise to build an index on this column. The running of one of the statistics gathering packages offered by most products, (Optimizedb for Ingres), would record in the dictionary that there are only two distinct values for this column, and under these circumstances the optimiser would disregard any index built on that column.

Example 2

Suppose we have the following:

```
SELECT ENAME FROM EMP

WHERE SAL = 3000

AND EMPNO = 7902;
```

If we have indexes built on both columns, different RDBMSs will use them in different ways. In general terms there are two alternatives. Firstly, it is possible to retrieve two data sets using both indexes, and then to merge them to eliminate those that don't satisfy both criteria. Secondly, it's reasonable to choose one of the indexes to drive the query and, for each row returned, check it to see if it matches the second criterion.

Oracle, for example, may use the merge technique in the above case under the following circumstances:

❑ The indexes are non unique

❑ The predicates are equalities (they obviously are in this example)

❑ The predicates are on the same table (again this is clearly so).

If the indexes are of different types (unique and non-unique), then Oracle may decide to drive the query from whichever predicate has a unique index. It is wise to remember that the methods chosen by the RDBMS to satisfy these types of query may change between different versions of database software.

Example 3

In most systems the following query:

```
SELECT * FROM EMP

WHERE JOB = 'MANAGER'

AND DEPTNO > 10;
```

will be driven by any index on the JOB column because few systems can use multiple indexes for 'bounded range' predicates.

Example 4

In the example:

```
SELECT * FROM EMP

WHERE DEPTNO + 0 = 20;
```

the addition of the '+ 0' will almost certainly stop the use of any index in most systems, and can thus be deliberately used in certain situations, to suppress index use.

These examples should give a flavour of how the optimiser works for you or against you in selecting the correct access paths to the data. In general, and whilst on the subject, there are a few guide lines that can be used.

Indexes will not usually be used where:

❑ There is no WHERE clause

❑ The predicate modifies the indexed column (by function or operation)

❑ The search is explicitly for rows with NULL or NOT NULL specified in the predicate.

Join Processing

Let's start by clarifying what I mean by the term 'join processing'. A join in SQL occurs when data is selected from more than one table in a single command – in short, where the FROM clause nominates more than one table (or the same table more than once). Just as there are many ways to write the same join query there are many ways, as you'll now realise, to execute it and the optimiser should be planning five things:

❑ Which primary indexes can be used

❑ Which secondary indexes can be used

❑ What order should the tables be joined in

❑ Which join method should be used

❑ Which locking strategy to use.

For evaluating join plans efficiently, it is absolutely essential that the utilities to collect data statistics are run on the columns nominated in the WHERE clause. Although I have not gone into detail about statistics collection, the optimiser should have at its disposal, both the number of rows in each nominated table, and the number of distinct values in the join columns. Some products – the Teradata DBC is a particularly good example – can also provide minimum and maximum values by column, and a kind of histogram describing the distribution of the data values in pertinent columns. These factors contribute to the high performance attainable on most join operations with this product.

There are four common join plans used by todays products, three of which are useful, the fourth, which I am going to describe first, being something to avoid if possible.

Cartesian Products

The simplest way to execute a join between two tables, is to firstly join every row in one table to every row in the other, and then from every resultant composite row, delete the ones not required. This is exactly what a Cartesian product is, and it can be easily produced, amongst other ways, by forgetting to specify a WHERE clause specifically joining the tables.

```
SELECT * FROM TABLEA,TABLEB;
```

will do the trick.

If table TABLEA has 100,000 rows and table TABLEB 400,000 then the Cartesian product will have 40,000,000,000 rows in its result set, so it should be clear why they are not a good idea.

Product Joins

Similar in outline to the Cartesian product (and not supported in some products), this is a very simple operation, used when there is no condition of equality specified. Every qualifying row from one table is compared to every qualifying row in the other so potentially again, there could be large overheads where both tables are large.

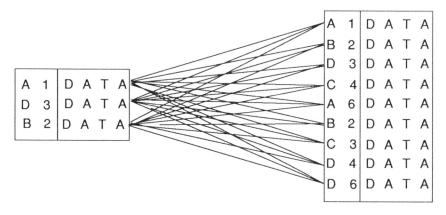

Figure 10.1 A Product Join

Sort/Merge Joins

Used when tables are of similar size, or when the join condition is based on equality, each table is accessed and rows selected that match any WHERE condition. The qualifying rows are then sorted and merged with each other, with rows without counterparts in both tables being discarded.

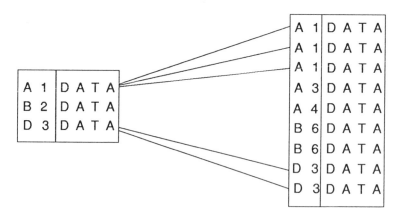

Figure 10.2 A Sort/Merge Join

Primary Index Look-Up (Nested Joins)

In the case of an equi-join between a large table and a small table, or when there is a WHERE clause that is highly selective, it is quick to simply select the qualifying rows from one table, and perform direct look-ups into the other (SELECT from the small table and look-up into the large one) Of course this look-up will only be quick if there is a usable index in place, hence the name Primary Index Look-up.

Just as the optimiser needs to select the most reasonable join plan for a specific query from the strategies described above, it also needs to decide which order to process tables in if there are more than two nominated in the query.

To clarify the issue look at the query:

SELECT ... FROM A,B,C,D where .....

The tables can be processed in one of two ways, as shown in Figure 10.3 below.

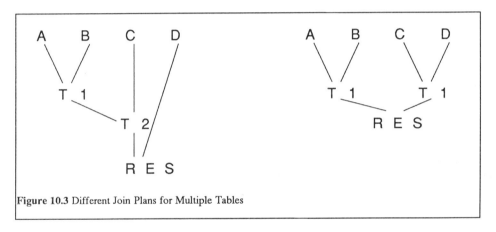

Figure 10.3 Different Join Plans for Multiple Tables

Now, if our query carries a WHERE clause that includes nearly all the rows from Table D, and there are a lot of them, then our first method may be preferable because there is only one join operation with that table, whereas the second method involves Table D in two joins.

So, the life of the optimiser is certainly a difficult one, and it is a subject of great competition between the RDBMS vendors. Because of this, it is difficult to obtain any information about exactly how each functions in the different products. Because the query execution plan is so important there are three questions you should be asking:

1) As a user, can I see the plan before it is executed on my behalf?

2) Is it possible to alter the way in which a query is executed by the way I write the SQL?

3) Is it possible to impose resource limits on queries to trap the odd rogue Cartesian product or very large query?

Dealing with the third question first, I don't know of a product that allows this type of control at present, and there are no moves to incorporate such a facility in the SQL standard. It is certainly seen as a desirable facility, and is likely to be implemented in most leading products in the near future.

I'd like to be able to answer a firm 'no' to the second question above but it's not possible at present. With older versions of Oracle for example, it was certainly possible to effect the order in which tables were presented in join operations, by simply changing the order of their nomination in the FROM clause, and there were all sorts of other tricks available to the knowledgeable programmer. A good principle to employ, is to write SQL to eliminate rows from the selection as early as possible so that the query:

SELECT JOB,AVG(SAL) FROM EMP

WHERE JOB != 'PRESIDENT' AND JOB != 'MANAGER'

GROUP BY JOB;

will in general be more efficient than the same query when expressed as:

SELECT JOB,AVG(SAL) FROM EMP

GROUP BY JOB

HAVING JOB != 'PRESIDENT' AND JOB != 'MANAGER';

It's also possible to help execution, in some cases, by adding redundant information, a trick that I've seen illustrated by the following example in DB2:

SELECT * FROM STAFF,DEPT

WHERE STAFF.DEPTNO = 104

AND STAFF.DEPTNO = DEPT.DEPTNO

AND DEPT.DEPTNO = 104;

In this query, the last line is redundant but may allow DB2 to use an index on DEPT.DEPTNO to filter out all non 'CLARK' rows prior to the join.

So we come at last to the first question, and the answer to it is that some products do allow you to see how a query is to be executed and some don't, and I think that is how the situation is likely to stay in the near future.

Even within the products that do provide this facility, there is a range of user friendliness which is surprising when you think just how critical it is to be able to evaluate the likely performance of both *ad hoc* and production SQL statements prior to their execution. Of the big guns, Oracle, is the most unfriendly because it provided no reasonable facilities in this area for the user until version 6. DB2 provides EXPLAIN and trace information; but perhaps the best two examples currently, are the Ingres QEP facility and Teradata's EXPLAIN.

In short, it is possible to turn QEP on before running an Ingres query and the execution of the statement will by postponed; instead a diagram of how the query will be executed will be displayed. It certainly takes some effort and ability to read these QEP's especially when the SQL is long or complicated, but the information gathered includes:

❑ The order in which the table joins are performed

❑ Which indexes are going to be used

❑ How many rows are to be involved at each step

❑ Estimates of global CPU usage and I/O activity

❑ The type of joins involved.

Even better than this stylised plan is the one provided by the EXPLAIN extension to Teradata's SQL. Prefixing an SQL command with EXPLAIN, again suspends execution of the actual SQL statement, but this time, rather than a difficult to understand execution diagram, a full description is produced, (in reasonable lay-mans English), on how the statements are to be executed. This includes all the information above, but also with estimated elapsed timings for execution of each processing step (the DBC is a Parallel processing computer).

The next two figures show examples of the Ingres and DBC offerings, and serve to conclude this chapter which covers one of the most interesting and competitive aspects of relational database management systems.

Summary

1) The optimiser is one of the most critical facilities in the RDBMS simply because for nearly every SQL command there will likely be several possible execution paths. Some of these may be orders of magnitude better than others.

2) Optimisers should be transparent to the user in as much as the user should not be able to directly affect the way in which they operate.

3) It should be a central function to ensure that the optimiser has sufficient information on data distribution and index availability to do its job efficiently.

4) It is important that facilities exist to examine QEPs for response time diagnosis and capacity planning.

```
select i.cuactno from dummy d, ibcuact i
        where d.cuactno = i.cuactno and i.cuactno = 300640

                no stats

|cuactno        |
|_____|

                                Join(cuactno)(CO)
                                Sorted(cuactno)
                                Pages 1 Tups 1
                                D25 C0
                /                               \
                Proj-rest               dummy
                Sorted(cuactno)         Heap
                Pages 1 Tups 1          Pages 47 Tups 1630
                D1 C0
/
ibcuact
Isam(cuactno)
Pages 59 Tups 1630
|           300640|
|           300640|
|_____  |
(2 rows)
continue
```

Figure 10.4 An Ingres QEP

```
explain select sale_type, region from base_table, store
        where dept = 50
        and sale_date = 880801
        and item = 5
        and store.store = 10
        and store.store = base_table.store;
```

Explanation

---

1) First, we do a single-AMP JOIN step from {LeftTable} EXPL.store by
    way of the unique primary index "EXPL.store.store = 10.
    "with no residual conditions, which is joined to {RightTable}
    EXPL.base_table by way of the primary index
    "EXPL.base_table.SALE_DATE = 880801,EXPL.base_table.DEPT = 50.
    , EXPL.base_table.ITEM = 5.,EXPL.base_table.STORE =
    EXPL.store.store" with an additional condition of (
    "EXPL.base_table.STORE = 10."). {LeftTable} and {RightTable} are
    joined using a nested join. The result goes into Spool 1, which
    is built locally on that AMP. The size of Spool 1 is estimated to
    be 160 rows. The estimated time for this step is 2.43 seconds.
-> The contents of Spool 1 are sent back to the user as a result of
    statement 1. The total estimated time is 2.43 seconds.

Figure 10.5 A DBC Explain dialogue

11

Transaction Management

The very concept of a DBMS, be it relational, hierarchical or any other manifestation, is of a pool of data managed largely by a set of central software, namely the DBMS itself. The quality of the data held, in terms of integrity, consistency and recoverability, is a large responsibility of this software and these are subjects that will be expanded upon later. For now let's consider three things that we would expect of our system:

1. We would hope that the data always makes sense. It must not be possible, for example, to hold data about an invoice line if we hold no record of an invoice for that particular line.

2. We would hope that the data would be consistent in value so that the same item, when referenced in different parts of the database had the same data value. If two users ask for details of Jon Smith's age then they must always both get the same answer.

3. We would expect the data to be up-to-date, which means of course that it should also be recoverable after a crash.

A considerable amount of complex code, which forms a large part of the DBMS, is needed to satisfy these wishes. Although the points listed above may seem, to the casual reader, to be fairly independent requirements, to fulfil all of them requires, amongst other things, that the DBMS understands and manages transactions.

Basic Principles

In an attempt to remain as simple as possible, this chapter aims to explain the fundamentals of transaction management, and point out the facilities that should be available to implement transactions successfully. A fundamental requirement to achieve this successfully, is a safe and uncompromising locking strategy in all but the simplest of single-user systems. However, for the moment, and with the goal of simplicity in mind, we will assume that our database is single-user only and in the next chapter we will expand the scenario to that of multi-user capability when talking about concurrency problems in the RDBMS and locking in particular.

The basics of transaction management are very easy to understand, but often seem to cause confusion, so let's take a simple example as an illustration. Suppose we have a system which has a requirement that whenever a row in a master table (MASTERTABLE) is updated, a record is also written to a log table (LOGTABLE), recording both the username and time that the update to the master table was performed. We thus have two activities to perform on the data for every master table row updated:

❑ Firstly we must update the MASTERTABLE row

❑ Secondly, a row must be inserted into the LOGTABLE.

It's possible that these actions will be coded to run either asynchronously (independently of each other) or synchronously (one after the other) in a program with little concern to the order in which they are actually executed. Consider what happens however, if a failure of some type occurs after one of the actions has completed, but the other hasn't. Although the database will probably remain unscathed after the failure has been corrected, the data will no longer be current or logically correct. There may either be no log record written to record a successful update action, or a spurious log record may have been written recording an update that never actually happened, or more correctly, simply never got recorded in the database. Either way the integrity of our data has been compromised.

In real life, database activity is rarely this simple, so it is worth devising a more realistic example to show the importance of transaction management. Suppose we are designing a banking system and we have a program that updates a person's bank account and then debits that same amount from a different account – a procedure representing a simple transfer of money from one account to another. Whilst this program is running and executing these credits and debits, any failure of the program or machine, may result in a credit being completed without a matching debit, resulting in a lucky client and an out-of-pocket bank.

On the other hand, a debit might be executed without its matching credit, in which case the bank becomes even richer at the expense of a client. Either way the whole bank accountancy data becomes corrupt and unreliable.

The point being made here is that both these examples are of typical transactions – the fundamental concern being that, if any part of a transaction is executed successfully, then the whole transaction must also complete successfully. Obviously it must also be true that if any part should fail, then the whole transaction should fail so that it can be retried in its entirety.

You may commonly hear that a transaction is a 'logical unit of work', and such a definition serves well in our database environment. The ability to define and manage transactions is an absolute must for any computer-based system performing update, insert and delete activity, and certainly such management will be expected in an RDBMS. You will not be disappointed to learn that comprehensive transaction management facilities exist in all the better known RDBMSs although some offer different perspectives and strategies than others.

How Are Transactions Managed?

The simplest transaction possible is one supported by default in most RDBMS's, and that is the single SQL statement. If we decide to give everyone in our company a 10% pay rise we might update our employees' data with the following SQL command:

    UPDATE EMP SET SALARY = SALARY * 1.1;

This may take a little while to complete as it updates every row in our employees' table with their up-graded salary figure. If we had a machine failure whilst the statement was executing and the job aborted, it would be difficult to know which employees had been allocated their salary rise and which hadn't. Well, the truth of the matter is that this single statement as it stands, is handled as an implicit transaction. This means that if the statement does not successfully complete, then all the changes made to the data up to the point of failure are 'backed out'. All the rows that have been changed will be changed back to their original values so we know that no employees have been given the rise, and the statement can be executed again.

Let's now say that, in order to fund the salary rise, we're going to fire all our salesman so we run the following two SQL commands:

    UPDATE EMP SET SALARY = SALARY * 1.1;
    DELETE FROM EMP WHERE JOB = 'SALESMAN';

With no transaction management facilities in action, if the system fails during the update statement, then the result will simply be that no one gets a rise. However if the failure happens during the delete command then no salesmen will be fired and instead they will all receive pay rises – not quite what we had in mind! Further complications arise depending on what caused the failure in the first place. If it was a trivial failure during the update, then most systems will back out any completed update statements, and will then proceed with the delete without retrying the update, so it pays to understand how your system handles such disruption.

So what is the answer? The management at single SQL command level, as so far described, is common to all systems and is quite correct in its working, but in our second example we wish to ensure that either both commands work to completion, or both fail. To do this we must bind them both into a single transaction, and there are two common methods.

The non-standard method:

```
BEGIN TRANSACTION;
statement;
statement; etc
END TRANSACTION;
```

The ANSI standard:

```
statement;
statement; etc
COMMIT
```

Using the standard approach, a logical unit of work (transaction) begins when the first SQL statement is encountered, and builds up with the addition of others, until one of the following occurs:

```
COMMIT
ROLLBACK
Any DDL command is issued
error condition
logoff activity
abnormal termination
```

After one unit of work ends, the next executable SQL statement will automatically start the next, and so on. If there is no COMMIT or ROLLBACK statement in a program, the scope of the transaction will be the program itself and normal termination of that program will COMMIT the transaction in progress at termination.

COMMIT and ROLLBACK

When a transaction that involves the altering of data is being executed, then prior to physically changing that data a copy of it is written to a 'safe house' in its unchanged form. In Oracle Version 5, this is a function of the single Before Image file and it is the BIW process that performs these writes. In Ingres, each user has his own journal that records such changes and in the Teradata system, each disk has its own transient journal. At the end of the transaction the user COMMITs, and if all goes well, the transaction finishes and the correct results of it will be permanently recorded in the database. As there is no longer any need to retain the 'before images' of the data, they are erased. Note that no matter which scheme is in place, all data changes are made permanent at COMMIT time, and can no longer be removed without considerable effort.

If however, some sort of exception condition causes a failure mid-transaction, or the user in an interactive session enters ROLLBACK, because he no longer wishes to keep the results of the transaction, then the system will try to back out all changes so far made within this uncompleted 'unit of work'. To do this, the system will go to the file containing the Before Images of the data that has so far been changed, and write these to the database over the changed pages of data. This in effect, deletes all the changes recorded from that transaction so far. Such activity is called 'rolling back the transaction' and should be an automatic function of the RDBMS recovery function.

A fundamental difference in the architectures of Oracle and Ingres, at least up to versions 5 of each, is that whilst Oracle implements Before Image support centrally for all users, Ingres supports it on a per user basis. The Oracle approach, whilst seeming to have two definite disadvantages, namely the introduction of a possible bottleneck and single source of failure, it does provide support of what is called 'read consistency'.

Once again, let's see the sequence of events when an Oracle user updates data but then changes his mind:

1) User Y selects data for update from Table X within a transaction — Oracle copies the selected data from X to the BI file

2) User change data in Table X — Oracle writes the changed data to database

3) User Y realises he has make a mistake and issues a ROLL-BACK — Oracle retrieves the original data from the BI file and writes it back to the database over the updated data

This simple example shows how ROLLBACK works, but let's use it to see what 'read consistency' is. Suppose in our simple example above a further user, Q, attempts to read the same data in Table X whilst user Y is changing it. There are three alternatives:

1) Table X is locked by Y to all other users thus preventing anyone reading data, under these circumstances Q is locked out.

2) User Q reads data that is changing and may not even be committed. This may or may not be acceptable to Q.

3) Read consistency is implemented by some other mechanism, enabling Q to read the data in its form previous to X's changes.

In fact the presence of a central BI file enables choice 3 to be implemented, and instead of user Q reading data from the database and thus running the risk of seeing invalid or changing data, the read request can be diverted to the BI file thus ensuring that the data read, truly represents that held on the database at the time of the last successful commit.

Such read consistency requires both the equivalent of a Before Image file and for it to be maintained centrally. In actual fact, later versions of Oracle dispense with the

Before Image file and attempt to retain the before images of changed data in memory instead. Obviously this improves access time to such data but must have an adverse effect on the efficient use of memory.

So far the examples and explanations given have largely focused on a 'single user database', a situation that is unlikely if one moves out of the world of PC usage. In fact, RDBMSs are almost entirely, in practice, multi-user, and transaction management takes on a great deal of importance under these circumstances. In order to illustrate possible problems in the multi-user environment let's examine three classic cases of how perfectly good transactions can interfere with each other if left to their own devices.

The Lost Update

Suppose two users retrieve the same row at the same time, and both update it to different values. The final value of the row will be the value set by the user who COMMITs last, because in committing, the other user's update will have been overwritten.

	USER A	USER B
	retrieves 100	retrieves 100
time	updates it to 200	
	commits	updates it to 300
		commits

After these actions the final value of the row will be 300 and in effect, user A's update has been totally lost.

The Uncommitted Dependency Problem

Suppose now that user A retrieves a row, value 1000, in a transaction and updates it to 2000, but does not COMMIT. User B then reads this row which now has a value of 2000 and himself adds 1000 to it setting it to 3000. Unfortunately, user A now decides to ROLLBACK his transaction and so the row is set back to 1000 and user B's update has now been lost.

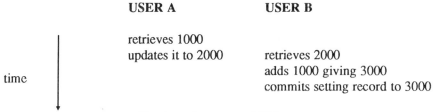

	USER A	USER B
time	retrieves 1000 updates it to 2000	retrieves 2000 adds 1000 giving 3000 commits setting record to 3000
	rollback setting row to 1000	

User B's update is completely lost.

The Inconsistent Analysis Problem

Imagine an SQL job is running to sum a money field in a table holding accounts data. Imagine also that running concurrently with this job is another one performing transactions of the nature already discussed – crediting and debiting pairs of accounts. Although the activity of the second job has no overall effect on the computed sum that will be the result of the first job, the degree of inaccuracy in the final result will depend on how this job progresses through the rows.

Imagine the table:

ROWNO	TOTAL
1	4
2	6
3	100
4	34

Suppose we have two tasks, the first of which is adding all the TOTALs (Task 1) and the second is going to subtract 2 from Row 2 and add 2 to Row 3 (Task 2). Logically the action of Task 2 should not effect the computed total returned by Task 1, but let's see what might happen if we're unlucky.

	Task 1	Task 2
time	Read Row 1 giving 4	
		Subtract 2 from Row 2
	Read Row 2 giving 8	
	Read Row 3 giving 108	
		Add 2 to Row 3
	Read Row 4 giving 142	

You will see that Task 1 has computed a sum of 142, but if you add the rows yourself you will get 144!

Such *concurrency* problems pose serious threats to the integrity of data held in multi-user database systems and the solution in all common systems comes in the form of sophisticated *locking* systems which are the subject of the next chapter. Before moving on to this subject, let's examine one further subject in which the term 'transaction' is gaining eminence.

Transactions Per Second

The formation in August 1988 of the Transaction Processing Performance Council (TPC), brought together all leading vendors of commercial computers, and several leading database suppliers, in an attempt to define standards, primarily in the area of database transaction performance. Such vendors included DEC, Unisys Corp, Hewlett-Packard Corp, NCR Corp, Tandem Computers Corp, Data General Corp, Teradata, Sun Microsystems Inc, Oracle Corp, Informix Software and Sybase, and so represent a formidable task force indeed.

Their goal is largely aimed at providing methods to allow different transaction management systems to be compared fairly in the arena of performance, because at present, and the discerning follower of benchmark results will, I'm sure, agree, such benchmark results mean next to nothing. We have in fact arrived at the unsatisfactory state of being subject to all sorts of various benchmark results, from different vendors, which in fact tell us nothing. They are almost universally difficult to understand, impossible to relate to real life, invariably designed to show the various products in their best light and almost always, because of the above 'features' absolutely worthless. So what can be done about this?

Firstly, we have to recognise that it is impossible in reality, to define a single benchmark test that can be used both to compare two different database products directly, and to illustrate the full range of functions that a multi-purpose database might be expected to support. However it's also not possible to give up at this stage because vendors need some performance related figures to release to potential users otherwise marketing may become a major problem. A first task of the TPC is likely therefore, to involve the definition of a transaction based test that under most circumstances can be used as a benchmark, and it seems likely that the famous Debit/Credit benchmark will be targeted for this purpose. For this reason, I have included this discussion in this chapter.

The Debit/Credit transaction has many of the earmarks of a successful standard OLTP test and its requirements have been available publicly since 1985. A common variety of it, the TP1 benchmark, was primarily designed to test hardware performance specifically to determine the maximum transaction rate that could be supported, with the restriction that 95% of the transactions should complete with sub-second response time. Communications overheads and 'think time' were also included, but these have largely been removed when using TP1 as an RDBMS performance measurement.

Let's look at the TP1 transaction in some detail, because in many ways it represents a stylised yet typical example of a transaction. The TP1 benchmark application represents a simplified banking system that tracks the account balances of a bank's customers at the account, teller, and branch levels. The data structures required comprise of four tables:

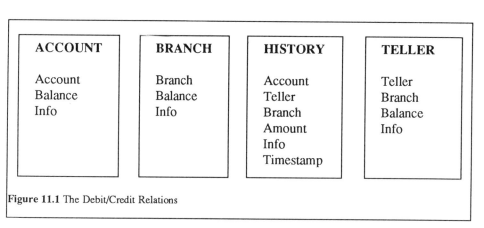

Figure 11.1 The Debit/Credit Relations

The transaction itself consists of three updates and a single insert:

```
Begin transaction
Update Account
Update Teller
Update Branch
Insert into History record of activity
End transaction
```

The size of the database is adjusted to the transaction rate of the system being tested in a ratio of 10 branches for each TP1 transaction per second that the system is expected to be capable of. A system that is being required to process 300 transactions per second should have, therefore, a target database of precisely 3,000 branches, 30,000 tellers and 3,000,000 accounts. This scaling can be a little hard to understand but is justifiable in the context that high throughput systems generally are based on large volumes of data, and conversely low TPS systems often only have low data volumes. In this guise the TP1 benchmark is aimed at checking whether a DBMS can fulfil its expected work rate, rather than providing definitive methods of comparing databases for the sake of it.

There are a great many rules that need to be carefully defined and adhered to in this sort of activity, as you can imagine. A number of TP1 and Debit/Credit tests have been performed with only one tenth of the required data volumes, and typically smaller volumes of data will always, in software based systems at least, yield disproportionately good results when greater portions of data can be held in memory and index levels are kept low. Don't forget that sort performance is not linear, and so small volumes of data can be sorted disproportionately quickly.

Hopefully, the definition of a transaction and its importance is now clear. It is best thought of as a database 'unit of work', and its organisation and execution is of fundamental importance. Because of its status it has also been, fairly unsuccessfully, used as a measurement of database performance, a topic that has been covered in Chapter 6, which explains the fundamentals of OLTP. However, and as already mentioned, transaction management is largely impossible without methods to control concurrent access to data and this is the subject of the next chapter.

Summary

1) Fundamental to all update processing, is the concept of a transaction being not only a unit of work, but a recoverable unit of work.

2) Transaction management should be transparent to the user, managed by the RDBMS, and usually defined by the applications programmer, or more satisfactorily, some centralised data administration.

3) Transactions vary in complexity, frequency of execution and criticality; but all share the same fundamental concept as 'units of database work'.

4) Standard transactions are being increasingly used as measurements of database performance.

References

Wiorkowski and Kull, Concurrency Control and Recovery in Database Systems *Addison-Wesley*, 1988

12

Locking

A primary concern of any database management system, as has been stressed previously, is how to control concurrency, or the accessing of the same data by more than one user at the same time. Without adequate concurrency control, data may be changed improperly or out of sequence, and as we have already seen, the consequences of this can be disastrous and very hard to identify, let alone correct.

Most database systems, including all the common RDBMSs tackle the concurrency problem by a strategy called locking. Broadly speaking, this means that if an object of data is selected to be changed, then no one else is allowed to change it for the duration of that original alteration - a 'lock' is applied to that object as it were. Although all systems as mentioned use a system of locking, there are many variations in how it is done, and so this chapter introduces some of these different mechanisms, and the consequences of using them, illustrating both their advantages and disadvantages.

Tackling Concurrency

Fundamentally there are two types of lock used in Relational Database Management Systems – the *exclusive* – I shall refer to this type henceforth as 'X', and the *share* lock which I shall call 'S'. We should also bear in mind that whilst users can explicitly lock objects in most systems, it is a prime function of the RDBMS to handle all locking considerations on behalf of the user and therefore, prior to any database activity - actioning an SQL statement for example, the RDBMS will take out whatever locks it deems fit to protect the database.

To help understanding at this stage, let's use a simple example in which I will assume that locking is done at row level. If user A starts updating a row of data, the RDBMS will place an X lock on that row so that user B for example, who might also wishes to update this same row, will be forced into a wait state, until user A COMMITs the changed row. When user A does in fact COMMIT his change, and the change is successfully completed, user A's X lock will be dropped and user B will be granted his own X lock on the row to perform his update. User B will now be presented with the new value of that row (which of course, may now not be a value he would wish to update). Thus the use of the X lock in this case serialises the update of the row, ensuring that user B sees the row as it was after user A had updated it.

If user A is merely reading a row then the RDBMS will give him an S lock on that row. Now if user B wishes to update that row whilst A is reading it he will require that the RDBMS grants an X lock on that row to him. This however cannot be done whilst the S lock is in effect, so user B again goes into a wait state waiting for user A to finish with the row, thus dispensing with the S lock enabling B to get his X lock required for update. It's simply a matter of queuing for the granting and releasing of locks.

If user B only however wished to read the row then it is permissible for him to get an S lock on that row whilst A also has an S lock – they can both read the same row at the same time, and this is the essence of a share lock (S).

Now we should have a basic grasp of locking, so let's return to the three consistency problems described in the previous chapter about transactions, to see how locking helps.

The Lost Update

In this example, both users successfully read the same row because both only require S locks, and two S locks on the same row can be granted with no problem. However, when user A tries to update he will require an X lock which cannot be granted due to the existence of user B's S lock, so A will enter a wait state. Unfortunately, when user B tries his update he meets with the same problem and both users end up in a wait state, each waiting on each other to perform an act that neither is being allowed to do. This is *deadlock* and is discussed later, it represents a serious problem in this strategy, but at least the database has not been corrupted.

	USER A	USER B
	retrieves 100	retrieves 100
	granted S lock	granted S lock
time		
	tries to update	tries to update to
	to 200 but can't	300 but can't get
	get X lock	X lock
	enters wait	enters wait state
	state	
		DEADLOCK

The Uncommitted Dependency Problem

Remembering back, this problem is illustrated when user A reads a row and updates it successfully but does not COMMIT. User B then reads the changed but uncommitted row and updates it further, only for user A to ROLLBACK his change, thus leaving the row in its original state with user B's update lost. Locking avoids this lost update because, when user A performs the original update he is granted an X lock on the row thereby stopping user B from acquiring either an S to read, or an X to update. In fact, user B will enter a wait state until user A's update is completed, when user B will see the updated version on which to perform his own update. Again consistency is maintained. In this example, A rolls back his update.

	USER A	USER B
	retrieves 1000 granted S lock	
time	updates 1000 to 2000 S lock escalates to X	tries to retrieve 1000 enters wait state
	rollsback setting row back to 1000	
	X lock dropped	successfully reads 1000 granted S lock

The Inconsistent Analysis Problem

Again going back to our example, as user A reads through the accounts table he will take out an S lock on each row as it is read. These locks will remain in place until the sum operation across the whole table is complete. User B therefore will not be able to update any row that has already been read by user A, and because User B's debit/credit activity is itself bound within a transaction, as soon as any activity is attempted by B on a row already locked by A, user B will enter a wait state. Unfortunately because B may also have succeeded in placing an X lock on a row that A has not read, it will only be a matter of time until a deadlock occurs when A attempts to read this X-locked row.

To illustrate this let's use the same example as in the previous chapter:

	TASK 1	**TASK 2**
	read Row 1 = 4	
	S lock on Row 1	subtract 2 from Row
time		2 X lock on Row 2
	read Row 2	
	can't get S lock	
	enter wait state	try to subtract 2 from Row 1
		can't get X lock
		enter wait state

DEADLOCK

Deadlocks

It is an unfortunate fact that such locking systems tend to produce many deadlock situations in highly concurrent environments. Two examples are given above, but any scenario that has the underlying strategy illustrated below will be vulnerable to deadlock.

	Transaction A	**Transaction B**
	lock a (X)	
		lock b (X)
time		
	attempt to lock b	
	wait	
	wait	attempt to lock a
	wait	wait
		wait

DEADLOCK

Most people imagine that deadlocks can occur only in multi-user, multi-statement transaction environments, but this is certainly not the whole truth. In fact we have already seen it to be possible for a user issuing just a single command (the update all rows in a table statement) to become deadlocked through the activity of another user. Some systems offer protection against this and Ingres for example, in such single statement transactions, allows all required locks to be preclaimed by issuing the command:

    set nodeadlock

Unfortunately it is possible when using some RDBMS's to achieve a deadlock situation in a single-user environment which can be quite alarming, but usually locking mechanisms can be turned off for such occassions. In short the pertinent points to remember are that:

1) The RDBMS should automatically detect and resolve deadlock situations, and this should happen most usually by aborting the transaction that has done the least work. Some systems abort the transaction that started most recently, and this is not, by any stretch of the imagination, necessarily the same thing.

2) In interactive sessions, the time that the system will wait on a lock should be tunable by the user of that session. The user should be able to instruct the system either not to wait on locks at all, and simply return an error message; or to wait for a defined time limit, after which it will 'timeout' if the lock has not been granted.

   Ingres provides the 'set lockmode' for just this purpose of specifying such a timeout period. If the timeout period is exhausted, then INGRES error 4702 is returned, and it will be the programmer's responsibility to handle this exception condition.

3) There should be facilities in any application code to handle deadlock in a friendly manner, to allow perhaps the automatic retry of a request that has been timed out, or to ask the user whether he wishes to wait on a lock, or do some other task.

4) During the course of a transaction containing more than one SQL statements, most systems accumulate locks on an 'as needed basis' – the alternative, to preclaim all required locks, is not commonly implemented. However, locks are not usually released until a transaction completes, even though they may not be actively required, and in some systems locks are not released in the event of a transaction being 'rolled back'.

5) The RDBMS should support implicitly, all locking activities on the data dictionary, or other objects it uses to manage the system. Such locking is essential to the running of the system, and includes such tasks as:

   a)   Locking the dictionary when any operation affecting it is executed. For example, when an index is created on a table, the dictionary may be locked until the tables in it, that record index-linked data, are modified successfully. This is the Oracle 'Dictionary Operations Lock'. It is also likely that the table being indexed will also be locked, but this is not what I am referring to here.

   b)   When DDL statements are being executed to change, for example, a table definition, it may be important to lock out any user attempting to execute an SQL statement against that table. In Oracle this is the roll of the 'Dictionary Definition Locks'.

c) Similar to the converse of the above, when a user is executing an SQL statement against a table, it would seem reasonable to lock that table against any user trying to perform a DDL statement against it. Imagine user A reading a column in a table whilst the DBA attempts to drop the table! This is the roll of the Oracle 'Table Definition Locks'.

Of course no RDBMS can offer full data protection by the use of only exclusive and shared locks, and in fact it's debatable whether any RDBMS manages at this point in time, to lock purely at row level, so there are two major areas to investigate, the second of which is a real bone of contention amongst RDBMS vendors.

Locking Granularity

My simple illustrations so far, have been based on a system which is capable of placing locks at row level, which is arguably the ideal level of granularity to which all systems strive. As I mentioned above very few, if any, vendors have achieved this yet, and at present there are different levels supported by different vendors.

Database level locking

In some systems which support the existence of many 'databases' within a single 'system', it is possible to lock complete databases explicitly. This might be done to make them momentarily unavailable to all other users, perhaps for backup or other maintenance work. This type of locking is not really what this chapter is concerned with but is included for the sake of completeness.

Table level locking

Whenever a user starts accessing a table, shared locks will be taken out to prevent another user altering that table definition, or in fact deleting the table in its entirety. A table level lock (X or S) may also be granted when the system decides that it is more efficient to lock the whole table, than to take out many row locks.

If for example we were to run the following SQL:

UPDATE EMP SET SAL = SAL * 1.1;

then the system would probable not take out row locks on every row as it is processed (thus running into the likelihood of deadlocking as illustrated earlier), but would simply attempt to place an X lock on the whole table for the duration of the update. It should be noted that the placing of locks does take processing time and memory and although the overhead is tiny, it can be significant, especially where there is a limit on how many locks can be outstanding at any one time (the VAX environment for example).

Page Level Locking

I refer here to a page being the physical unit of disk I/O for a particular system. This has significance in the Ingres RDBMS because it also represents the lowest level of locking granularity attainable. Generally a page will hold more than one row so that when a user tries to change a row, the lock he is granted will, in fact be taken out for every row in the same page. This may be a drawback when row length is small, but if only one row fits into a page, then we effectively get row level locking.

Row Level Locking

As I've already said, this is the optimum granularity for locking, but as yet is not widespread. Some systems come close to it and probably one of the best is found in the Teradata DBC system. Based on the fact that all rows are hash distributed in the DBC multi-disk system, locking is done at row hash level, which is effectively row level, unless more than one row hashes to the same value. Coming close to this level of granularity is Oracle (its non-OLTP version), which can offer true row level locking within transaction boundaries, but, at least up to and including version 5, this can be a little misleading so let's have a closer look at the Oracle case.

Row Level Locking Supported By Oracle (V5)

In addition to exclusive and share locks, Oracle supports an extension called *share update mode* which, in effect, allows it to implement row level (exclusive locking).

Share update mode is invoked within Oracle in one of two ways:

Explicitly

By using SQL extensions:

a) SELECT * FROM EMP WHERE NAME =
   'SMITH' FOR UPDATE OF SAL;

   or

b) LOCK TABLE EMP IN SHARE UPDATE MODE;

Implicitly

By accessing rows through the Oracle Forms or IAP systems.

This facility can be very useful in applications where a number of rows are being updated before a commit is being entered – typical of a forms-based application; or in fact where many other users are updating rows in the same table. If any user has a table locked in share update mode, then all other users must be in that same mode to perform insert, update or delete operations on that same table. The reason why this scenario, although to be commended, is not reflective of true row level locking, is because, even in share update mode, no two users can actually update a table physically at the same time. At COMMIT time, the table is locked exclusively for the use of one specific user, and so physical updates still serialise.

Locking Modes

We have already mentioned three common locking modes, namely:

❑ Exclusive

❑ Share

❑ Share update (Oracle only)

It is worth keeping in mind that the RDBMS will take these locks out on behalf of the user, and change automatically between modes where required. There is a fourth and common mode, which I will call 'access mode' that deserves a mention on its own.

Access Mode

We have seen a case where a user is reading many rows in a table to do a sum operation, and we have also seen that this operation interferes with any other user performing any type of update on that table. Imagine though that we wished to create a report across large amounts of data whilst the same data was subject to on-line update during the very period we wished to interrogate it. The locking modes defined so far, will ensure that both activities cannot be supported concurrently because we might be reading data that is actively being changed. Now, suppose for example, that as far as our report goes, we are not concerned that it is one hundred percent accurate, so it might be quite acceptable to run both the report and the update jobs concurrently. If we were looking for a single sum from a balance sheet, for example, we might not care what transactions were occurring, because each credit would have an equal and opposite debit associated with it, thus on average we could expect an answer close to the truth.

Most RDBMSs will support such activity, but the way in which it is done is quite different.

Teradata DBC/SQL for example supports the above mentioned 'Access' mode as an extension to its SQL:

```
LOCK TABLE EMP FOR ACCESS SELECT SUM(SAL)
FROM EMP;
```

Ingres uses its SET operator:

```
SET LOCKMODE ON EMP WHERE READLOCK=NOLOCK;
```

or
```
SET LOCKMODE SESSION WHERE
READLOCK=NOLOCK;
```

And Oracle merely ensures that when the report job comes to read a block that has been changed, it is diverted to the Before Image file where it reads the original data values prior to such change.

As I've been at great pains to mention, the RDBMS manages lock modes automatically, but it is important that facilities exist for the user to override and default locking, to enable his own requirements to be enforced. Thus in most 'varieties' of SQL, vendors supply extensions to enable the user to specify which type of locking to employ; so Oracle for example supports these constructs:

```
LOCK TABLE XXX IN SHARE MODE;
```

```
LOCK TABLE XXX IN EXCLUSIVE MODE;
```

```
LOCK TABLE XXX IN SHARE UPDATE MODE; or
SELECT ... FOR UPDATE
```

Ingres allows user-controlled locking by use of the SET command:

```
SET LOCKMODE SESSION WHERE LEVEL=TABLE
```

This ensures that, for this whole session all locks are taken at table level, and therefore the problem of escalation will never occur:

```
SET LOCKMODE ON tablename WHERE LEVEL=TABLE
```

```
SET LOCKMODE ON indexname WHERE LEVEL = TABLE
```

Lock Escalation

To illustrate an interesting feature of a certain locking strategy, I am again going to use Ingres version 5. I would however like to stress that it is by no means the only product to exhibit this 'feature'. I have already mentioned that the lowest level of granularity at which Ingres locks, at least up to and including version 5, is at page level where a page is generally a 2048 byte chunk of data. Because locks are a predefined resource within an Ingres system, the system itself attempts to automatically regulate its allocation of them. If a user updates many rows in a single transaction for example, there will be a lock granted for each page as its data is changed, and this can become expensive on this particular resource.

In order to regulate the supply of locks, if the Ingres Query Optimiser estimates that an activity is likely to require the locking of ten or more pages of data, it will forsake page locking and immediately try for a table level lock. If, however, it cannot make this initial decision, when a user has caused Ingres to take out more than 10 page locks on his behalf, the system will attempt to take out a table level lock, thereby enabling it to reclaim 10 page level locks – this is 'lock escalation' and this value of 10 is tunable by the SET LOCKMODE command to specify MAXLOCKS.

A query with no WHERE clause, or a range specification, will almost always force a table lock, unless Ingres's statistics gathering facility, Optimizedb, has been run previously on the table, and indicates a preference for page level locking. We have covered the subject of overflow previously, and its relevance here is that if a query references a row in overflow, then many pages of that overflow chain may require locking for just one request. This might well result in escalation to table level locking.

Even worse than this is a situation that can occur in some operating systems of which VAX/VMS is an example. Lock management of Ingres under VMS is actioned by VMS's own Lock Manager and as such, this facility, as well as Ingres itself, has its own quota of locks that can be outstanding at any time. If either of these quotas becomes dangerously depleted, then Ingres will try to recover locks by escalating from page to table level locking.

So what is the problem in automatically escalating from page to table level locking?

Suppose user A is running a query that causes such escalation, whilst user B is also updating the same table. User A will wait, because he will be unable to obtain the exclusive table level lock he requires to proceed, because B will have outstanding X locks. Now supposing user B's update activity causes his job to escalate to table level locking, then he too will wait on user A and we have a classic deadlock situation. By the very nature of this situation, one user stands to lose some work which may be of some considerable volume. The lesson is, lock late, commit early.

To conclude therefore, locking is one of the most significant aspects of an RDBMS, and although different products facilitate it in different ways, it is not always easy to pick out the best methods. Certainly to support OLTP applications, row level locking will become a must because, in any systems supporting large numbers of users, the efficiency of concurrency management becomes one of the most telling issues.

Summary

1) Fundamental to transaction management within an RDBMS is a fail-safe and automatic system of resource locking. Such a strategy should be transparent to the user; comprehensive; and efficient, but should provide users with some ability to turn off or override default mechanisms.

2) Locking should be done at the lowest level of granularity possible, and at present the goal for all vendors is to implement true row level locking without the need for escalation.

3) Automatic locking often forsakes performance for security, and it is often necessary to specify explicit locking requirements within applications. Where this is necessary it should be done with the greatest of care, remembering that it is, of course, a major part of physical database design.

References

Bernstein, Hadzilacos and Goodman, Concurrency Control and Recovery in Database Systems *Addison-Wesley,* 1987

13

Access Control

I have started other chapters with a reminder that a primary requirement of a Database Management System is to be able to hold a large variety of data, perhaps from many different sources. This chapter points out that it must also be capable of managing different levels of user access to that data securely, efficiently and sensibly. In all but the simplest of applications, it will be the case that different data will be required by different users, and that the control facilitating access to data in such a discriminating way, should be administrated centrally.

An odd effect of databases is often that of dehumanising data, and of removing people's identity with data they formally regarded as their own. Tight security and access controls go a long way to restoring that identity, which in general tends to be a helpful aspect.

This chapter shows two different approaches to the administration of such control, pointing out possible consequences of each.

Selective Security

A major function of a DBMS must lie in controlling the accessibility of the data it holds, in terms of the major SQL operations SELECT, UPDATE, INSERT and DELETE, and under which circumstances, and by whom, they can be used. Obviously applications software has an important part to play in any such restrictions, but such code should not be expected to take on the whole responsibility, because it can in no way restrict direct user access through any of the 'user tools' provided by the vendors. Control must therefore be available at RDBMS level and exercisable centrally. In order to plan for selective security, we must recognise that the different types of user requiring access to a database fall into several categories:

❏ The Database Administrator will possibly have access to all data within a facility, or more likely, all the data in an occurrence of a database.

❏ The application user, whose activity is defined purely by controls exercised within the application, will most likely use subsets of data, unaware of any controls limiting his activity.

- The application developer may or may not have free range within the confines of a development database.

- The 'computer-literate user', perhaps having a knowledge of local data structures, may use SQL for analytics and other types of *ad-hoc* query.

- The restricted user, who is only ever allowed to read certain data depending on its actual values and will be protected from accessing tables by a layer of controlling Views.

It is quite likely that an individual person may be any or all of the above, depending on what he is doing, when and in which database. To satisfy the above requirements there must be at least two levels at which access must be controllable. These two levels lie at the operating system interface and in access to the RDBMS itself.

Operating System Access Control

In general all database users will gain access to the database environment by first logging onto the machine that hosts the database. At this level, access will be controlled very carefully, by the resident operating system, and a username/password combination will be expected that will not only give access to the computer, but will also associate that particular user with a profile of privileges assigned to him for the duration of the logon session.

It will be most unusual to find an environment where this is not so because it is this mechanism which is fundamental, in most cases, to the security of the whole machine. It is also unlikely that following a successful logon, a user will be left at an operating system prompt to do whatever comes to mind, but there will undoubtedly be times when for whatever reason it does happen. To safeguard against this, the DBMS should create its own internal files, especially those comprising the database, in such a way as to ensure that they are protected certainly from deletion, and preferably from read/write access except through 'proper channels'.

Database Access Control

In most cases, a database will simply be a resource on a computer available to certain applications or users, and it will be common to find that there are other applications and file handlers on the same machine. Whilst the operating systems username/password protects the computer from unauthorised access, a further level of protection will be required on the database itself, to ensure that the population of database users remains under the control of some central database authority.

Just as users log on to machines, many databases insist that users also log onto the database environment itself after having successfully accessed the operating system. Thus, just as the operating system holds a list of authorised user with their privileges, the DMBS itself will include some mechanism of holding the names and privileges of the users enabled to use the database. Typically this information will be held in the databases' dictionary.

Both Oracle and Ingres allow the DBA full control over user access to databases, but interestingly enough both choose very different methods.

The approach chosen with Ingres very much mirrors its strategy of encouraging the creation of multiple subject-oriented databases. When Ingres is initially installed, a database called DBDB, is created in order to hold certain data about all other databases created on the system. This database will be owned by the default Ingres user called 'INGRES' and, by means of a utility called **Accessdb**, all other users are made known to the installation and their level of privilege defined. Accessdb is itself a forms-based system that will allow the Ingres master-user to logon to the DBDB database, and create entries to associate potential new users to the Ingres system, with their required level of privilege. It is plain that this differs greatly from the Oracle approach. Whilst Ingres defines users as being 'able to use the Ingres installation', Oracle defines them only in association with the ability to access specific databases, as we shall see later.

As briefly mentioned, a function of Accessdb is to assign certain privileges to a user and the two most relevant privileges are the ability to create databases and the ability to become a **'superuser'**. Let's look at these a little closer.

Alongside two system-created users who have some global authority, namely System and Ingres, other users may or may not be able to create databases, depending on privileges assigned via Accessdb. This is significant in as much that the creator of a database becomes its DBA, and automatically attains a role of responsibility and authority over that structure. This becomes particularly relevant to the lower levels of security defined later. The superuser facility, when assigned to a user, enables that user to mimic any other user (including DBA and superusers) thus giving free range over the installation. Superusers can, for example, define other users to Ingres and assign them similar system wide privileges.

By default, all Ingres databases are accessible to all users, although the data in such databases is not. It is important to realise that when a user logs onto such a 'public' database, no objects owned by other users will be accessible, without the express authorisation of the DBA of that database, who alone has the ability to allocate objects as shareable by taking ownership of them himself. As a further level of control, it is possible to define a database as private, and such an assignation restricts access to the database to a select list of users.

Ownership of Ingres items (databases, tables, forms etc) is, therefore, closely dependent on operating system defined usernames and privileges granted by the Accessdb utility. This mechanism is reasonably comprehensive but is undoubtedly geared toward control at the installation/user level.

Oracle contrasts sharply with this, by implementing a security strategy dependent mostly on the database itself; a strategy evolving clearly from the fact that the database in Oracle is seen much more as a single entity supporting many applications and users than in the Ingres scheme. Just as, at installation time, Ingres defines a privileged user called Ingres who owns the installation, each Oracle database at installation inherits two user definitions, these being known as **Sys** and **System.** The two do have slightly differing roles, but the detail of this distinction need not bother us here. Suffice to say that Sys and System are both classified as Oracle DBAs and thus have the authority to allow other users to access the database.

A further difference is illustrated here. In Ingres, access privilege is given to a user via his operating system username, but in Oracle there need be no association between the operating system user name and that defined to Oracle. To illustrate this difference let's use an example of a user called Fred. If Fred is to access an Ingres database called X the sequence of events will start with the computer system manager firstly defining Fred to the operating system, to give him access to the machine hosting the database. Let's say this access is associated with a username of FRED and password BLOGGS. Now an authorised Ingres superuser, using Accessdb must nominate FRED as a *bona fide* user of Ingres and define his privileges on database X. Once these tasks are completed, Fred can access database X by first logging on to the machine (username = FRED, password = BLOGGS) and then typing X SQL X to create himself an interactive SQL session on X.

In Oracle, the fundamental difference is that Fred does not need an account of his own. In fact the only task that needs to be performed to give Fred access to X, is that an authorised Oracle DBA must define Fred to database X using the SQL GRANT command. This is because Oracle has its own username/password requirement for logging onto any database so that Fred, once he has got access to the machine using any available user account, can only access X by nominating it and supplying the username/password specified by the GRANT command.

At this point we should note two things. In Ingres, all access rights are defined and recorded centrally within the single DBDB database, whilst with Oracle every database contains its own access information. Secondly, access to an Ingres database is not directly password controlled whereas with Oracle it is.

Controlling Privilege

The factors controlling user privilege are defined by two layers of commands, of which the SQL layer is the most common between products, and the most detailed. However, on top of this common layer, are facilities in each RDBMS that have no counterpart in the other, so it's wise to describe these here.

Just as Ingres allocates the DBA and superuser facilities to users by Accessdb, it can also authorise specific users to use trace diagnostics, and be able to update the dictionary tables. This second feature can be useful, but is also inherently dangerous, although the ultimate update, the ability to drop a dictionary table, is not possible in either RDMBS. In general, the ability to use the tracing facilities are only useful to development staff, and the ability to update dictionary tables should be disabled for all, and be controlled strictly by the DBA. Oracle has its own security enhancements which are allocated as extensions to the standard SQL GRANT command thus:

```
GRANT CONNECT/RESOURCE/DBA TO username
[IDENTIFIED BY pass word];
```

The functionality of this command is threefold. It defines user <username> to the database from within which the GRANT statement has been issued. It gives this username a password controlling access to this specific database, and lastly it defines the level of privilege this user has on this database. In summary these levels of privilege, which are Oracle extensions are:

Connect   With this privilege a user can create views and synonyms but cannot create tables or indexes.

Resource   A resource user can create all objects and can GRANT or REVOKE privileges on owned objects to others.

DBA   A DBA user has full access to all data and facilities.

In effect the granting of a DBA privilege to an Oracle user is comparable to the same level of status in the Ingres system. However, there is no concept of a 'Connect' user in Ingres, so let's examine this a little closer. The greatest restriction to the connect user is the inability to create tables, and this can have major advantages under certain conditions. Consider the end-user who is allowed access through SQL to production data. This type of user may qualify for Connect only, so that access to data can be tightly controlled and the ability to create data tables removed. In a similar vein, an application may run from a connect-only user if the application does not create tables. In general this is a very desirable state of affairs, but in reality applications are often forced to create temporary tables during execution, particularly for the creation of complex reports, or to make up for some of the short-comings in some versions of SQL.

The above-mentioned privilege level assignment within the Oracle GRANT statement is an extension to SQL, and is unlikely to be found in the standard definition of SQL. However, it is likely that some support for the concept of a **public** table will be provided and this is, if you like, a global switch that makes a table accessible to all database users. It is a very handy facility and is achieved by Ingres by ensuring that any table to be publicly accessible, is owned by the DBA of that database, and the relevant **permits** on it are defined.

Function Control

Already we have seen how it may be possible to restrict users to certain functionality, depending on levels of privilege, by using either the SQL GRANT command or other command extensions. However, SQL includes many more comprehensive facilities to control functionality, at the level of specifying the ability of specific user to execute the major SQL commands, namely:

❑ SELECT

❏ INSERT

❏ UPDATE

❏ DELETE

A simple example which will give Jones read access to the EMP table is:

GRANT SELECT ON EMP TO JONES;

In order to give everyone all possible privilege on the same table one could use:

GRANT ALL ON EMP TO PUBLIC;

The granting of such privileges should work in such a way that an owner of a table has the ability to pass on permission, to perform operations on his tables, to other users, who might themselves to some extent, pass these permissions down to others. Thus 'permissions hierarchies' might be formed following the rule of course, that permissions can only get more restrictive as one descends the hierarchy.

Data Restrictions

A further security requirement takes the strategies defined above and increases their power by allowing the restriction of specific users at both column and data value in that column. This means, for example, that it is possible to restrict user Bob to accessing only records from a central, multi-column company payroll file, that belong to himself. This would be done by issuing a GRANT statement such:

GRANT SELECT ON SALARY TO BOB WHERE EMPNAME = 'BOB'.

Thus from a full company-wide salary table, even if Bob typed:

SELECT * FROM SALARY

he would only get as a result:

EMPNAME	GRADE	SALARY
BOB	B	50

In the Ingres environment, one could further restrict access to particular times of the week, through use of its extended syntax. This is very powerful stuff but one shouldn't forget that such access, to a large degree, can also be controlled by ensuring that base table access is performed through views. In many ways, this represents a preferred approach.

The facilities to control access to data managed by the RDBMS itself, are therefore both complicated and comprehensive. However do not forget that most users will not communicate directly with the data, because there will generally be a layer of applications code in place, so consider at all times the worth of implementing complex access strategies. Often strict and comprehensive security strategies become so intolerable that they are flagrantly ignored by the privileged, and thus become more trouble than they are worth, and an actual liability to security.

Summary

1) Comprehensive security facilities should be available, easy to control, implement and understand. They need not be complicated because the more straightforward they are, the more successful they are likely to be.

2) Applications are the front-line data access protection, so application control should be compatible with database restrictions at all times. In many ways database security protects the data, whilst applications-based security protects the user.

3) Consider the performance overheads. Complex views, permits or other involved security mechanisms may well be expensive on CPU power at the time the query is parsed and executed.

4) Consider the differences required to support logon in batch or interactive modes. Often batch jobs have to use hard coded username/password combinations, which is far from satisfactory.

5) A last word when evolving a strategy of access control which is of importance. When a request for data is refused due to an access restriction should the user be notified or not? This is a question of some importance and some dispute. Some products will not signal the user of a violation, but simply return no data; whilst others will post an error message under such conditions. Both strategies have some good and bad points – it is for the user to decide.

14

Data Integrity

The word 'integrity' is defined in the dictionary as 'honesty, wholeness and soundness', but in the world of the database it can be interpreted simply as ensuring that the data stored in a database always makes sense. Certainly the subject of data integrity has become such an important one in the competitive RDBMS market that a chapter on the subject must be included in this book, even if only to clarify what it is, how it may be ensured, and its importance.

Unfortunately, in many cases the concept of data integrity has been confused with just one aspect of the subject, namely referential integrity. However, it should be remembered that referential integrity constraints on their own are not enough to guarantee that a relational database is kept in a sound state. There are at least five different types of integrity constraints that must be considered, and must interact together to preserve the 'wholeness and soundness' of the database.

Integrity Constraints

Let's start this chapter on integrity constraints by listing the five types which, logically at least, should apply to a database. These constraints are:

❏ Domain constraints

❏ Entity integrity

❏ Column constraints

❏ User-defined integrity checks

❏ Referential integrity

Although some of these are interrelated, for ease of understanding it would seem wise to explain each one in isolation.

Domain Constraints

Before progressing with an explanation of domain constraints it is imperative that the concept of a domain is understood. Briefly, a domain in relational terms, is the set of all unique values permitted to appear in one or more specified columns, coupled with some sort of identification of the objects or properties which these values share. To clarify this explanation let's use a simple example. Suppose we have a column in a table, called DAY-OF-WEEK and it is defined as a character string of length 10. It's reasonable to presume that the only possible values that this column can hold are:

Monday
Tuesday
Wednesday
Thursday
Friday
Saturday
Sunday

If we give this list a name, say DAY-NAMES, then we could define a simple rule that says that not only must the contents of DAY-OF-WEEK consist only of characters and be less than 11 letters long, they must also only be selected from the list called DAY-NAMES. In this example DAY-NAMES is a *domain* and DAY-OF-WEEK is in the domain of DAY-NAMES. Thus if a user attempted to insert the value 'montag' into this column, it would violate the domain constraint and be rejected, even though it conforms to the Char 10 datatype description defined for the column DAY-OF-WEEK. The relevance of domains in relational databases is highly visible, because all join-type activity between primary and foreign key values should match data drawn from the same domain.

In the following simple example, we should see that the CURRENCY column in both tables must contain values drawn from the same domain, and that domain itself represents a list of all the valid CURRENCY identifiers that have been defined in the world of finance. We are not saying here that the CURRENCY column in the ACCOUNT table must never have a value that is not found in the CURRENCY column in the RATES table (however this is true in this case but is subject to a different type of constraint), but rather that the CURRENCY column in both tables must only hold values drawn from a clearly defined and finite range of values.

ACCOUNT	RATES
ACC-NO AMOUNT CURRENCY	CURRENCY XCH-RATE

In most implementations of relational databases however, domains remain just a concept, but there is good reason to have them enforced centrally by the RDBMS with their definitions being held in the data dictionary. There would be two requirements:

❑ Some method to define the domain in terms of its name and description, a CREATE DOMAIN command perhaps.

❑ Some method of associating columns with domains. This could be done by extending the CREATE TABLE statement for instance.

The benefits of such support lie mainly in removing likely sources of error from the applications programmers, and putting responsibility in a centralised role. This should lead to very sizable productivity improvements indeed and reflects the fundamental database concept yet again. In addition, support of domains may allow the implementation of domain-based indexing techniques which have proved of considerable worth in prototype models. Domains could even be useful by removing the possibility of user errors occurring when columns, which are not logically equivalent are joined mistakenly.

Entity Integrity

This requirement is stated clearly in E. F. Codd's 12 relational database rules outlined in Chapter 7. In short, it is enforced by ensuring that the primary key of a relation, or any column constituting part of it, can never take a null value. Most relational systems do allow the use of a column constraint (see below) which can be used to ensure that a specific column can never take such a value, but this is different from having a rule which not only defines the primary key but enforces that no part of it can be null. The former method will remain prone to error, whilst the latter should be foolproof, but depends entirely on database support for the definition of a primary key.

Column Constraints

The value in any column of any table should be controlled by column constraints, which are defined for that particular column, and recorded, once and only once, in the central data dictionary. Such constraints should be expressible, without involving value from other columns, or they may involve the comparing of values from columns with the target rows of the constrained column. An example of the first type shows how Teradata implements column constraints:

```
CREATE TABLE PERSONNEL(
    EMPNO SMALLINT BETWEEN 1000 AND 9999,
    BONUSNO SMALLINT BETWEEN 0 AND 99 NOT NULL,
    BONUSAMT DECIMAL BETWEEN 1.00 AND 5000.00);
```

This is a simple implementation, which suffers from the drawback of not allowing any check against actual values in any other columns. Ingres supports the creation of integrities by use of the DEFINE and DESTROY INTEGRITY commands which do provide, in a limited way, such functionality. For example the EMPNO restriction above could by implemented with the command:

```
DEFINE INTEGRITY ON EMP IS
     EMP.EMPNO > 1000 OR EMP.EMPNO < 9999;
```

Such integrity constraints have the advantage in that they can reference other columns so:

```
DEFINE INTEGRITY ON EMP IS
(EMP.SAL < 2000 AND EMP.DEPT = 'ADMIN')
OR
(EMP.SAL > 2000 AND EMP.DEPT = 'SALES');
```

User-defined Integrity Constraints

This type of facility allows business rules to be applied centrally to the database, so that when a certain action is performed on a set of data, other actions are automatically triggered, conforming to some user-defined and centrally recorded set of rules. In general terms such facilities are implemented as *triggers* and take the form of a sequence of three types of definitions:

❑ Define the condition which actions the trigger

❑ Specify the test to be made

❑ Specify the action to be taken if the test fails.

An example lies in the use of a trigger to prevent an account being overdrawn. Using this simple example, the condition that we which to test for might be any change to the balance figure held for an account. The test might be to ascertain, whether that account remains positive or goes negative, and to see whether that customer has already arranged overdraft facilities. The action will probably be to reject the transaction if it is likely to result in a negative balance, and no arrangements for an overdraft have been made.

The use of such triggered functionality is not widespread in the database community. Some products have implemented such facilities at applications level, but this does not address the issue sufficiently because the control and definition of such constraints must be done centrally. The code, I suggest, should reside in the data dictionary (perhaps even in compiled form?).

Referential Integrity

This is the most recognised type of integrity constraint, so is deserving of a more detailed explanation.

First of all let's see what referential integrity is, with the aid of an example.

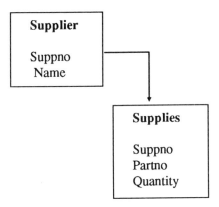

This is a simple data model of a one-to-many relationship between Suppliers and the Parts that they supply, using a notation that has been introduced earlier in this book.

In this example, if Supplier SMITH (SUPPNO = 100) dies, and his name is removed from the Supplier table, then in order to preserve the integrity of the Supplies table, any records of SMITH supplying Parts should be removed, by deleting all rows from the Supplies table that are related to Smith, ie have a SUPPNO = '100'. This is simply because if Smith is no longer with us, he can hardly be expected to continue supplying Parts except under the most exceptional of circumstances! Now this is not always the case as we will see later, but it is an example of a *bona fide* relational requirement that actually says:

> If a relation (Supplies) includes a foreign key (Suppno) matching a primary key (Supplier.Suppno) in some other relation (Supplier), then every value of the foreign key in that relation (Supplies) must be equal to the primary key in some row of the other relation (Supplier) or be wholly null.

In short therefore, this is the rule, which if adhered to, enforces what is known as referential integrity. All code, be it in an application or the DBMS, that enforces referential integrity, does so by applying referential integrity checks.

Although my example above is a case where referential integrity checks should be enforced it is a bad example on two counts:

1) We would certainly not wish Supplies.Suppno to ever hold a null value and indeed this would violate another relational rule, because Supplies.Suppno forms part of the primary key of a table and thus cannot, even in part, be null.

2) For some reason, we may well wish to hold data about Smith in the Supplies table even though he is no longer a valid Supplier.

Let's look therefore at the more reasonable and very common type of example from the world of finance that I used earlier.

Let's assume that we have the following two tables:

Account		
Accno	Amount	Currency
104	1024	USD

Rates	
Currency	Xchrate
USD	1.7

In this example the account table simply records account transactions holding an amount, in the AMOUNT column, and the currency in which the figure is held, in the CURRENCY column. The rates table holds up-to-date exchange rates for all types of currency being traded.

Suppose we have an application that inserts account information into the account table above. We might reasonably expect that when the currency value is entered a check is made against the rates table to ensure that the currency is valid, and indeed, this is a good example of a column constraint as described earlier. This relationship between the two tables, based on currency, is of utmost importance to the two tables. It will be used to convert amounts held in the account table, but held in various currencies, into sterling, by looking up the exchange rate (Xchrate) for that currency in the rates table. Supposing however, that the row from the rates table with primary key value 'USD' (United States Dollars) is deleted for some reason. The consequences of such action will be that any activity to insert a record with USD as the currency into the accounts table should fail, because of the column constraint violation, but unfortunately, any account record that is already in the table and in USD currency, will not be representable in Sterling because there will be no exchange data recorded in the rates table to enable the conversion. The data will be seriously compromised.

Of course, these problems are nothing peculiar to relational databases, and have previously been catered for by strict application coding. What is new to the database world however, is the possibility of holding such validation rules, not in application code, but centrally in the RDBMS itself.

This should be possible because we should be able to concisely define relationships between tables by nominating specific columns and either primary or foreign keys. Such referential integrity constraints defined through the RDBMS itself, should facilitate central control, and remove heavy burdens from the applications programs.

Before progressing, it's worth explaining a couple of terms. In the world of referential integrity the rates table in our example above is termed the 'referenced' table and the account table, the 'referencing' table. Inconsistencies can often happen when:

1) A row is inserted into a referencing table.

2) A primary key value is changed in a referenced table.

3) A foreign key value is changed in a referencing table.

4) A row in a referenced table is deleted (as in the case of our example).

To reinforce these points let me reiterate that, without the benefit of any centrally managed constraints, each individual application must be written in such a way so as not to violate any required referential integrity rules. In our example above, any program, that allowed deletion of a row in the rates table, would surely have also taken the steps to ensure that no account rows referenced that currency would be deleted. This requirement obviously places both a heavy work load and responsibility on the application teams, and of course *ad hoc* access to data, especially if available from any interactive form of SQL, could cause real problems.

So as already mentioned, the alternative, and this is the reason why this issue has become so important now, is to ensure that the RDBMS itself should both record relationships between objects defined within the database, and thus be able to enforce referential integrity constraints itself, as defined by a central authority (the DBA). For those concerned with this subject, it is worth examining some current ideas, and the likely ANSI standard, to see just where the industry is positioned at the moment.

In short there are three types of referential integrity rule being targeted at the moment for implementation within the RDBMS itself and each is described below.

Cascade Option

If a row in the referenced table is deleted, then all rows in the referencing table with a foreign key value equal to the primary key value of the row, should also be deleted. If the primary key value of a row in a referenced table is updated, all rows in the referencing table with a foreign key value equal to the primary key value of this row, should also be updated to the new value.

Set to Null

If a row in the referenced table is deleted, all the rows in the referencing table, with a foreign key value equal to the primary key value of this row, should be set to null.

Restrict

A row in a referenced table cannot be deleted if there are rows in the referencing table with a foreign key value equal to the primary key value of this row.

A primary key value of a row in the referenced table cannot be updated if there are rows in the referencing table with a foreign key value equal to the primary key value of this row.

These rules are by no mean exhaustive, and refer to relationships between two tables. Further complexity is introduced by what are known as self-referencing tables, described next.

Self-Referencing Tables

To illustrate just what is meant by a self-referencing table, and to show some of the hidden complexity of enforcing referential integrity checks on such structures, let's use the following table as an example:

EMP

EMPNO	EMPNAME	MANAGER
7566	JONES	NULL
7788	SCOTT	7566
7876	ADAMS	7788
7902	FORD	7566
7369	SMITH	7902

Figure 14.1 The EMP Self-Referencing Table

In this example table, we have the unusual situation where the column MANAGER can be thought of as a foreign key to the table's primary key which is EMPNO. Both columns are defined on the same domain, to use previous terminology. To illustrate the point let's consider the SQL required to list out the employee names, alongside the names of their managers. To do this requires the table to be joined to itself, an action not uncommon in the relational world.

```
SELECT A.EMPNAME, B.EMPNAME
FROM EMP A, EMP B
WHERE A.MANAGER = B.EMPNO;
```

Logically we can think of this query as using two 'copies' of the EMP table, joining them across EMPNO and MANAGER, a relationship in which MANAGER is a foreign key and EMPNO the primary key. We can consider it to look something like this:

Table occurrence 1		Table occurrence 2	
EMPNAME	**MANAGER**	**EMPNO**	**EMPNAME**
JONES	7369	–	–
SCOTT	7566	7566	JONES
ADAMS	7788	7788	SCOTT
FORD	7566	7566	JONES
SMITH	7902	7902	FORD

Figure 14.2 The Logical Join Across a Single Table

The point of this illustration is, that if in our EMP example we delete the row where EMPNO equals 7566, then the rows for employee SCOTT and FORD lose their integrity because their managers cease to exist. There is a clear requirement then for a referential integrity constraint in this example, across columns of the same table and such a constraint is termed a 'self-referencing constraint'.

Implementing Referential Integrity

Unfortunately at the time of writing this book, there are very few RDBMSs that include referential integrity checks, and so it is not easy to illustrate how they will look in code. DB2 appears at this time to be leading the way in this field, and has implemented extensions to the DDL set of commands, to define the types of relationships so far discussed. For example, to create a table with a referential integrity check which requires referencing another table may look something like this:

```
CREATE TABLE WORKERS
(WORKER-NO CHAR (8) NOT NULL,
DEPART-NO CHAR (3) NOT NULL
FOREIGN KEY DEPART-NO (DEPART-NO)
REFERENCES DEPARTMENT ON DELETE RESTRICT);
```

In this example, a relationship is defined between the WORKERS and DEPART-MENT table, whereby it will not be possible to delete a row from the DEPARTMENT table which has corresponding values in the WORKERS table.

A more complete example (not based on DB2) may look something like:

```
CREATE TABLE SHIPMENTS
(SUPPLIER-NO CHAR(4),
PRODUCT-NO CHAR(4),
QTY INTEGER)
PRIMARY KEY (SUPPLIER-NO,PRODUCT-NO),
```

```
FOREIGN KEY (SUPPLIER-NO IDENTIFIES SUPPLIERS,
    DELETE OF SUPPLIER-NO RESTRICTED,
    UPDATE OF SUPPLIER-NO CASCADE)
FOREIGN KEY (PRODUCT-NO IDENTIFIES PRODUCTS,
    DELETE OF PRODUCT-NO RESTRICTED,
    UPDATE OF PRODUCT-NO RESTRICTED);
```

Note here that I have incorporated the idea of the PRIMARY KEY clause in this example, an idea that was raised earlier. Interpreted in English, this means that in the SUPPLIER or PRODUCT tables, the delete operation is restricted to the case where there are no matching shipments. Any update to SUPPLIER.SUPPLIER-NO will also update any related SHIPMENTS records, but and update to PRODUCTS.PRODUCT-NO will be rejected.

Of course, it must remain true that if the RDBMS does not provide automatic RI checking then applications code must do so, and this has both advantages and disadvantages. If referential integrity is enforced by the RDBMS, then development productivity should increase because design should be simpler, fewer lines of SQL code will be required, and data should be more uniformly consistent and reliable. It's true that central implementation of referential integrity constraints can have unnecessary performance overheads, and these will often be difficult to ascertain or estimate.

User-enforced integrity checking can be useful to increase performance, especially when applications do a great deal of update activity or are time critical, but will generally leave a potential for data corruption, especially in an environment of large-scale update. It's likely, and probably essential, to have some mechanism of switching such integrity checks on and off, and the presence of them will necessitate the provision of certain tools for management. Such tools or facilities are likely to include:

1) The ability to switch RI checks off when loading data.

2) The ability to check tables for contravention of any RI rules.

3) The ability to rebuild tables that are in a corrupt state in terms of referential integrity rules.

4) The ability to report table dependencies and RI rules.

5) The ability to checkpoint and recover logically related sets of tables.

The Timing Factor

In order to introduce another area concerning referential integrity implementation, consider the following table update statement on this simple one column table:

INVOICES

```
┌─────────────────────────┐
│      INVOICE NO         │
│                         │
│          1              │
│          2              │
│          4              │
│          6              │
│                         │
└─────────────────────────┘
```

UPDATE INVOICES SET INVOICE-NO = INVOICE-NO + 1;

If there is a unique index on INVOICE-NO then the operation above will work only if the rows are processed in a certain order. If the row with INVOKE-NO = 1 was selected and updated to 2, then we would have a duplicate key value and the update would fail. However it would be theoretically possible to successfully complete the update on all records if they were processed in the order 6,4,2,1 because at any instant there would be no risk of duplicates. The point of this example is that, just as the success of failure of this update may logically depend on the order in which the rows are processes, RI checks are also prone to timing constraints and can be executed at one of three stages during the processing of a transaction:

1) In flight – the referential integrity check is made after each row of a set is processed.

2) End of SQL statement – the referential integrity checks are performed after the total target set of a single SQL statement has been processed.

3) At COMMIT time – checking is deferred until a complete transaction, which may consist of many SQL statements, is committed (or End Transaction reached).

From a performance stand-point it is usually preferable to perform the integrity checks in flight, but lets look at what can happen, bearing in mind the above example, with a simple self-referencing table having a Delete Restrict RI constraint.

EMP

EMPNO	EMPNAME	MANAGER
100	JONES	
200	SCOTT	100
300	ADAMS	100
400	FORD	NULL

DELETE   RESTRICT
Constraint

If we execute the SQL command:

    DELETE FROM EMP WHERE EMPNO > 250;

and there is the RI constraint as shown above, which means that it is not possible to delete an employee who is the manager of another employee, then there are two alternative results if referential integrity checks are made at the end of processing individual rows.

1) If the records are processed in the order of EMPNO = 300 then 400 the sequence of events will be:

   EMPNO 300 is a manager of EMPNO 400, therefore deletion is restricted

   EMPNO 400 is not a manager, so this record is deleted.

   Therefore the row where EMPNO = 400 is deleted.

2) If the records are processed EMPNO = 400 then EMPNO = 300 the sequence is:

   EMPNO 400 is not a manger, therefore the row is deleted

   EMPNO 300 is no longer manager of EMPNO 400 therefore this row can be deleted.

   Therefore both rows EMPNO = 300 and 400 are deleted.

These types of analyses provide some interesting insights and pointers to some areas of concern. To conclude, it seems that in-flight checks are likely to cause problems, so restrictions on the type of RI checks allowable with different types of processing are likely to be common place, a factor made especially pertinent when the order of rows processed by SQL is in effect, random.

To end this chapter, I would therefore like to stress the fact that the implementation of centralised integrity constraints, and their maintenance by the RDBMS, is likely to be a complicated and involved business, and will take on new levels of complexity in a distributed environment. I have not delved into it deeply, and there are many other facilities that will be implemented by different vendors in different ways. Two things however can be banked upon. Firstly, the relational database with its integrated dictionary facilities provides the very tool with which integrity can be defined and enforced centrally. Secondly, the vendors of relational products are going to provide quality facilities in this area as it becomes seen to be a facility providing major competitive advantage, to both vendor and user alike.

Summary

1) Although referential integrity is of key concern in the relational world, it is only one part of a larger field concerning data integrity. Users should not forget all the

other types which can often have greater impact on development, throughput and data safety.

2) Referential integrity is often poorly understood in theory, and the difficulties of implementing it grossly underestimated.

3) Domain integrity should be viewed with a great deal more interest than it is currently receiving. It is fundamental to some very important design issues.

15

Auditing

Auditing is a word that usually strikes horror into the heart of all concerned, except the actual Audit department. However, the scope of the term should be understood and the ramifications of it evaluated.

Auditing facilities are important in the database environment, not only to provide evidence to external parties that an application or system is performing in a predictable and acceptable manner, but also to provide internal information, which can prove extremely useful to such bodies as the DBA team in tracking down application faults, database anomalies, performance issues and user access violations. Information gathered by auditing facilities can also, if so desired, form a useful measurement on which to base accounting systems

What is Auditing?

We should accept that a DBMS is in fact responsible for all the issues raised in the introduction to this chapter, which in short means that it should record (or be capable of recording), all user access, all data changes and all resource usage within its environment. This sounds like a complex task, but because the DBMS of necessity 'sees' all transactions being executed against it as they happen, and knows on whose behalf they are being executed, it should be possible to easily and quickly implement a dynamic and complete set of centralised or distributed auditing facilities within our DBMS.

Firstly therefore, let's discuss what auditing means, because it is a subject often raised and discussed, but not often implemented in computer systems, be they database oriented or not.

In simple terms there are four requirements:

1) To provide a record of all user access to all objects of significance to the system.

2) To provide a record of all data changes during operation of the system.

3) To provide a record of all resource usage by a user.

4) To ensure that the detail above is available in readable form, and in a timely manner.

In a non-DBMS and non-4GL environment, the provision of these facilities can be very expensive in both design and program development stages, saying nothing of the extra machine resource required, which typically manifest themselves in extra I/O activity. The situation should change however, when we move to a RDBMS environment because the database manager itself knows about all auditable activity occurring on all data, by all users, as and when it happens. Recording it should not be that expensive. To provide comprehensive auditing facilities therefore, requires just two things – the logging to the database of all action as it occurs, and the provision of tools to make the information easily available.

It remains a constant surprise to me that even though we are dealing with facilities that are simple, at least in theory, to implement, very few of the currently available RDBMSs do a particularly comprehensive job. Still, although progress in this area is slow, some products are showing increasing awareness of this area of functionality. Oracle Version 5 for example, audits security type operations quite comprehensively, although at present, it does not audit data changes themselves in sufficient detail. Ingres on the other hand, does a fair job in allowing the auditing of data changes, but doesn't choose to log security-related information as comprehensively. It falls to Teradata to provide extensive resource usage data, but perhaps this simply reflects its position in the high-performance marketplace.

Why then, do I maintain that the task of providing auditing facilities should be simple? My thoughts are three-fold:

1) All activity against a database involves accessing the dictionary tables to check access rights of individual user to perform specific tasks. It would seem a simple job to log all such activity to separate 'activity' dictionary tables.

2) The provision of transaction rollback capability and journalling facilities, described elsewhere in this book, requires that when a data row is changed by an update, or a table's data content is changed by insert or delete, detail of those changes is recorded either in transient journals or permanent logs.

3) RDBMSs invariably provide 4GL-type products which can easily be used to make audit data available with minimum expense.

It is worth now examining these areas more closely.

Security Auditing

As I have already mentioned, Oracle introduced auditing facilities in its Version 5 release, implementing them initially as a security feature. It does not record values of updated, inserted or deleted rows, but records primarily user activity on the database structure itself. By default, and this is common, all auditing facilities are switched off, but when switched on can service, in different ways, the auditing requirement of both users and DBAs.

A user may use SQL to:

❏ Select certain allowable audit options

❏ Control the level of detail recorded

❏ Choose to audit either successful or unsuccessful activity on his tables (or views) .

In addition, a DBA is able to:

❏ Monitor successful logon and logoff attempts

❏ Monitor usage of the GRANT and REVOKE commands used to allocate or remove privileges from users

❏ Set default options

❏ Enable or disable use of the audit trail table.

Unfortunately, auditing facilities are not, at present, subject to any real or useful form of standardisation, and so the SQL used to define requirements has to be a vendor specific SQL extension. The Oracle extension looks like this:

```
AUDIT        options
ON           table name
BY           ACCESS/SESSION
WHENEVER     [NOT] SUCCESSFUL;
```

A list of the 'options' includes:

```
ALTER, AUDIT, COMMENT, INSERT, LOCK, RENAME, SELECT,
UPDATE, DELETE, GRANT, INDEX.
```

To put this in context, an SQL statement of the order:

```
AUDIT INSERT ON JONSTABLE
BY ACCESS
WHENEVER SUCCESSFUL;
```

would cause entries to be made automatically into the system-wide audit trail table, every time a row was successfully entered into JONSTABLE. The audit trail entry would contain information including:

❏ An identifier of the user who perpetrated the insert

❏ An identifier of the terminal through which the transaction was entered

❏ The time at which the activity occurred.

❑ The type of transaction executed.

An interesting feature, although I'm not sure in reality if it is particularly useful, in the ability to write comments directly into the audit trail table using the Oracle function USERENV, which can substitute values for terminal type and session ID etc.

The above options are available to the user of adequate privilege but it should be remembered that it is the DBA who has overall control of auditing facilities. The DBA can enable or disable all auditing at Oracle Warm Start time and also has extended ability to allow auditing of all logon and logoff activity, certain activity of global concern (CREATE PARTITION for example), and a powerful facility to audit all activity that results in a 'does not exist' type error.

Data Auditing

In order to allow the auditing of action taken on the data itself there are two choices. Firstly it is possible to write a separate audit function within the RDBMS. This facility would be required to record both the before and after images of any updated row, and the contents of any rows involved in an insert or delete action. Of course, information, such as who and when, would also be required to make sense of the changes and attribute them to individual users. The second choice would be to utilise already existing RDBMS functionality; so let's look at the second option more closely because it would seem to be both more efficient and easier to implement.

In order to support transaction management, every user session currently executing SQL statements within a transaction, must have access to what I shall call a transient log (the Before Image file in Oracle terminology). Within this log, the before images of all rows that are being updated or deleted, within the confines of transactions, are kept, and for all records inserted, an identifier of some type is stored which can be used to identify that inserted row.

If the transaction does not complete, then this transient log is read sequentially, oldest record first, and all these before images, pertinent to the failed transaction, are written back to the database; and any rows marked as being inserted during the transaction are removed. On successful COMMIT, or after that type of recovery mentioned above completes, the transient log entries are deleted. If this facility was modified so that:

❑ The transient rows were not automatically deleted

❑ Select activity was recorded as well

❑ The new values of all columns changed were stored

❑ Full copies of any inserted rows were held

then the logging facility could be used as the basis of an audit file.

Unfortunately, this type of transaction management using transient journalling is of absolute importance to transaction-based systems, and the changes I have outlined might impose a processing burden intolerable to real-time OLTP systems (unless of course they themselves required sophisticated auditing facilities). OLTP systems often achieve their very small response time requirements by keeping transient logs permanently in memory because of their highly volatile nature, and changes as I suggest would make this impossible. So, what are the alternatives to using the transient logs?

As I've already mentioned in a previous chapter, Ingres, as a selectable option, offers After Image Journalling at both database and table level. This facility causes all data changes to be recorded in a separate sequential file, in case the original database should become unusable. If this should happen, the defunct data is deleted and replaced with that from the last security dump. The files to which all the changes have been logged are then read, and all the logged transactions applied serially to the database thus bringing it up to date. This is roll-forward recovery and the files recording the transactions as they are committed, are often termed After Image Journals. This is a subject covered in more detail in Chapter 11. The reason why this is of significance in the context of this chapter, is that when a record is updated or inserted, its column values are recorded in the After Image Journals along with identifying data, such as when and by whom the changes were made.

This is exactly the type of information required for our auditing facility, excepting the fact that once again SELECT type activity will not be logged. The advantage of the Ingres product is that the journal can in fact be made readable, using a facility called AUDITDB, and then copied into a database table for further manipulation or access by its 4GL tool set. So in this example, we have a very simple way of implementing some auditing facilities with no immediate impact on OLTP-type users who would probably be using the journalling facility anyway. However you will note, and I have already mentioned the fact, that no SELECT type activity is being recorded at any time and if this is a concern then some home produced code will be required.

Resource Usage Auditing

A third type of audit information that can be of some real benefit concerns resource usage by a user. When such information is coupled with the kinds of data mentioned previously, some very useful information can be extracted indeed. Some might argue that this is not an auditing requirement, and in the more traditional sense I would not argue, but choose to include it here for completeness. To expand, if we think of the user accessing the database, then there are two types of resource usage: that used by the RDBMS on behalf of the user, and that used by the user himself (I shall call this *host* resource). The ratio of host to DBMS's resource usage can vary tremendously, especially when the user retrieves or loads large amounts of data to or from the database. In the database machine environment, the definition between host and DBMS becomes very easy to understand, and so the following describes some of the mechanisms that such a machine, the Teradata DBC/1012, supplies automatically, to facilitate the auditing of such facilities:

- ❏ A log table is maintained of all Checkpoint, Restore, Rollback, Rollforward and Dump activities. This can be used to audit specific usage of such utilities by user and time.

- ❏ A log table is maintained which records all use of external magnetic media (tape) for the dumping of data from the Teradata DBC. The username, time, type of activity and tape volume identification information are all recorded here.

- ❏ All attempted logon activity is recorded by username and type.

- ❏ A history of all machine resource usage (CPU and I/O) is kept, entries being made at user-defined intervals.

- ❏ All activity resulting in changes to access privileges is recorded.

Because all the data noted above is held in SQL accessible dictionary tables, vast amounts of information can be gained for example, by joining the records of user access to those of resource usage. If one couples the ability of the Teradata to maintain both After and Before Image journals, then it should be possible to get close to a full auditing facility maintained automatically by the DBMS. Unfortunately SELECT activity is once again impossible to track down.

It seems therefore that we are likely to have to wait a little longer until full auditing facilities are provided within an RDBMS. I don't think the wait will do much harm, although it is probably unnecessary. Implementing full auditing facilities within an RDBMS will just add further processing and I/O demands, and when vendors are taking such pains to reduce these, it seems unlikely that they will be anxious to provide more facilities in these areas.

Summary

1) Nearly all systems that change data are likely to be subject to some form of audit requirement even if such a requirement is flagrantly ignored.

2) In the database world it seems logical to make the fulfilment of such requirements a central task, because the DBMS itself should at all times know exactly what is happening to the data it controls.

3) In general, such central audit facilities are poorly supplied by relational database vendors which is surprising because on inspection, it does not seem to be a complex task to undertake.

4) As different vendors target government departments as possible purchasers, we may see a greater concentration on the provision of automatic auditing facilities.

References

Fernandez, Summers and Wood, Database Security and Integrity *Addison-Wesley, 1981*

16

Backup and Recovery

With data volumes growing all the time, there is an ever-growing trend to increase the number of bytes stored per disk. Whilst just a few years ago, 96 Megabyte exchangeable disks were very fashionable in the mini-computer world we now see vast IBM 3880 technology supporting greater than 7 Gigabyte fixed disks. One can only guess to what extent this trend may reach now that optical disk storage is with us and commercially viable.

Whilst the technology improves however, disk crashes are still a problem that only the most optimistic DP manager will ignore, and it seems true enough to say that a disk crash will always happen at the most inconvenient moment – I wonder how much data has been lost (and its value) across the world of the uninitiated PC user! If we go to the other end of the scale and consider machines employing hundreds of disks in arrays, we find that overall machine mean time between failure (MTBF) figures are being measured in days – an alarming evolutionary trend to say the least. Clearly sophisticated backup and recovery mechanisms are required

When Things Go Wrong ...

Of course, whilst we must expect and cater for such events as disk crashes, they are largely out of our control, let us not fool ourselves into thinking that it is the only way we can catastrophically lose data. Consider the careless, unscrupulous or ignorant person who simply deletes data for some reason best known to himself, and we all know that there are a million ways to do this. So there are two major problems which might compromise our data so that it is either not available, not up to date or just corrupt. These are:

❑ Data lost through hardware problems or disaster.

❑ Data lost by human activity or application error.

Realising therefore that at any time it is possible to lose the database, either in its entirety, or any part of it, permanently, a mechanism is required to ensure that after any such loss the data can be recovered, either up to the time of the loss, or to some ime previously when the data was known to be in a consistent format. There are many mechanisms that can help:

1) A DBMS can be used which maintains a complete copy of itself on another disk subsystem so that the loss of one copy of the database simply initiates a swap to the other and an in-flight recovery of the lost version. This is an expensive solution in all cases, and is not one favoured by many current software RDBMS vendors. It has been used by some home-grown systems successfully, but is bound to put additional overhead on the hardware. Possibly the best example of this mechanism allows the Teradata database machine to survive multiple disk or processor failures by keeping a 'fallback' copy of every row in a table immediately accessible if its 'prime copy' should be lost.

   Be aware though, that this type of security does not protect the data against corruption by a user or an application.

2) An operating system is used, that performs the above function for all data on nominated disks. This solution is certainly of interest and is widely supported by many hardware manufacturers especially in the fault tolerant world. Disk shadowing has now been introduced in the world of the VAX VMS operating system, and when implemented can actually improve performance by allowing the retrieval of data from whichever disk (of the shadow pair) that will give the least seek and latency time. Again this type of security protects only against hardware faults.

3) Operating system utilities are used to periodically archive the database, usually to tape. This is the traditional method of data security within the DP fraternity, but it suffers from two major drawbacks:

   ❏ The database usually has to be quiescent during the dumping activity.

   ❏ It takes a long time to back up a very large database and traditionally the whole database has to be archived or restored at once, again a major problem if the database is large.

   Even taking these drawbacks into consideration it is likely that this type of activity will remain the backbone of security for a long while, especially for those establishments that require a copy of the database to be stored off-site for either security or disaster recovery requirements.

4) Software is used to periodically checkpoint, and then continually journal database activity until the next checkpoint, providing the ability not only to restore data as it was at the instant it was checkpointed, but also to 'roll the data' forward from the journals to bring it up to date. This is After Image Journalling.

As a generalisation, it is true to say that the major RDBMSs available today are very sound, and very similar in their solutions to the problems outlined above. This is certainly not a subject that reveals major advantages and disadvantages between products. This was not necessarily true in the earlier days when I remember diagnosing a major problem in the Oracle Version 3 After Image Journalling mechanism, which caused it to halt after writing 13 journals without any sort of notification whatsoever! This does highlight the need to test all new features with a certain degree of thoroughness and, although not directly related, it is wise to check entire security strategies once in a while to ensure their adequacy.

The major question raised when considering this area of functionality is how, where or if to use it.

Consider the database whose contents are refreshed entirely every night, for the use of Management Information Systems (MIS). Is it worth worrying about securing the data at any point? Almost certainly not and similarly, read-only data hardly need concern us as long as there is an off-line copy somewhere that can be used for recovery.

However, imagine an on-line transaction system, perhaps serving a network of automatic tellers, and further imagine the consequences of not being able to bring the data automatically up to date following a major data loss.

Recovery Facilities

As previously mentioned, there are several areas of functionality required from the database management system to enable full data recovery and these include :

❏ Dumping

❏ Restoring

❏ Checkpointing

❏ Journalling

❏ Roll Forward recovery – After Image Journalling

❏ Roll Back recovery – Before Image Journalling

The utility or utilities therefore, which action such activity, are likely to be fairly sophisticated. At the very least they should provide for the copying of the database, in a special format if required, to a safe data set that is located on different media than the one holding the original data (it is clearly nonsense to hold the backup copy on the same disk as the original). To do this they must have some sort of checkpoint facility, so that they can be certain of the integrity of the database prior to copying it: it would not be reasonable to copy an inconsistent version of the data. Taking a copy of the database is of somewhat limited value if there are no facilities to load it in place of a damaged copy. As far as recovery is concerned therefore, and again in the worst case, we would expect a utility that would replace the database in its entirety, as it was at the time of the checkpoint and dump of the original. This scenario has some major limitations:

❏ During checkpoint and dump, the database will usually be out of service to the user-community, and for a large database this may be some time.

❑ Similarly, recovery may take a long time and will not generally allow user-activity until completion of the whole database reload.

❑ The database will only be recovered up to the point at which it was checkpointed, not to the point at which it crashed.

A fully functional dump/restore facility however should allow:

❑ Checkpointing at the level of database, user, table, view etc as defined by the person performing the checkpoint.

❑ The securing and recovery of discreet parts of a database whilst others are actively in use.

❑ A mechanism to allow the data to be secured and recovered up to the moment of the crash.

As we enter an age of greater sophistication, there is clearly a requirement to move to such a sophisticated mode of operation, which would also be mandatory for both very large databases and those that are required 24 hours a day, 7 days a week. Smaller or non-critical systems however, can often make do with simple backup strategies without the bells and whistles, and the facilities can often be satisfied in almost every respect, by using whatever native dump/restore facilities are provided by the operating system.

A Recovery Sequence

Let's continue with examining how a sophisticated security strategy works.

On an active database, many users will be executing many different transactions, and all will be in a different state of execution at any given time of the day. Some data will be undergoing changes in memory, some uncommitted data will already be written to disk, and various users may be waiting to perform actions on various locked data objects. If no security features are active, a head crash on the disk housing the database will destroy it totally and forever.

To safeguard against this possibility, it is usual to take periodic dumps of the database interspersed with checkpoint and journal activity. Let's see how this works as a series of steps.

A Checkpoint is an activity that will make a copy of a database (or object in it) with a guarantee that the data in the copy is in a sound state – there are no half-committed transactions for example. The checkpointed data can be dumped to disk or tape, and forms a complete copy of the object at a given moment in time, with guaranteed data integrity. Between the taking of checkpoints, journalling can be used to record the results of every transaction that completes so that if a database is lost, a combination of reloading the dumped database and applying the journal entries, will bring the database back to how it was prior to the loss.

This type of journalling is called After Image Journalling and is actioned in the way described in the following list of activities, which attempts to illustrate the sequence of events in a full security and recovery cycle.

Security Cycle

STOP USER ACTIVITY
SWITCH JOURNALLING OFF
CHECKPOINT DATABASE
SWITCH JOURNALLING ON

user activity	DUMP CHECKPOINT
recorded in journals	DUMP SAVED JOURNALS
	DESTROY SAVED JOURNALS

STOP USER ACTIVITY
SWITCH JOURNALLING OFF
CHECKPOINT DATABASE
SWITCH JOURNALLING ON

user activity	DUMP CHECKPOINT
recorded in journals	DUMP SAVED JOURNALS
	DESTROY SAVED JOURNALS

etc......

However, supposing during user activity data becomes corrupt or the database is lost. With the above sequence of operations active, it should be possible to recover the database up to the moment it went down, with the exception of any transactions that were uncommitted at the time of the crash. These will be lost. The schematic for recovery is now:

Database goes down

SWITCH OFF JOURNALLING
DESTROY DATABASE
RELOAD DUMPED COPY OF DATABASE
APPLY JOURNAL ENTRIES
CHECKPOINT DATABASE
DUMP DATABASE
DUMP JOURNALS
DESTROY JOURNALS
START JOURNALLING

user activity
recorded in journals ....

This process of writing completed transactions to a journal, as I've already mentioned, is called After Image Journalling, and although widely used, it is implemented in different ways. Some products simply copy whole changed pages from memory to the After Image Journals, whilst others hold detail on a row-by-row basis which allows some degree of auditing activity, a feature discussed in Chapter 15.

The newer versions of Oracle use the same files maintained for transaction recovery (the Redo log) to create permanent After Image records, and this seems a particularly elegant feature.

There are a few things to be aware of:

❑ Single journals which service many users have the potential for bottlenecking

❑ Journals should not be kept on the same devices as real data

❑ Journals do contain valuable audit information but this is not often accessible in a useful format

❑ Journals will hold no record of SELECT type activity.

A very neat feature of some products, roll forward facility, is the ability to specify a specific time in which to roll forward to. This is useful because it implicitly provides the ability to roll back a database to some previous time, and such a feature can be used to remove the effects of a rogue transaction from the database even though it did in fact commit successfully. Most RDBMSs provide this timing facility within After Image Journalling functionality, a notable exception being Teradata's DBC which instead provides full user controlled Before and After Image Journalling.

To conclude this chapter, the subject of journal-related recovery is becoming of great interest as relational databases become larger and of more critical nature, and this is typically coinciding with their move into the demanding world of OLTP. Non-stop systems will have requirements which are unnecessary in 95% of installations, which can get away quite happily with fairly rudimentary, and therefore cheap, facilities. So the lesson is to base the security strategy of an installation on what is required and not on the facilities which are available.

Summary

1) All database systems which recognise transactions as fundamental units of work must support some form of roll forward database recovery activity, and the best will cater for rollback as well.

2) Specialised database machines or database products aimed at the OLTP market, must attempt to be non-stop, and will thus require sophisticated and automatic recovery mechanisms which will usually involve replication of data.

3) Database recovery should be planned, and the plan tested. Regularly securing large quantities of data is an expensive task, and it would be unfortunate if recovery from it was found to be impossible in a live situation.

4) Base a recovery strategy on what is required not on what is possible.

17

Data Dictionaries

A great selling point of RDBMS products has been their comprehensiveness in their provision of 'Integrated Data Dictionary' support. I'm sure however, that if you asked a handful of people just what it is they think such an facility is, you would get many different replies, not only regarding what an IDD should contain, but also its importance. In this chapter I'd like to explore the idea of dictionaries and where they originated from. They are of importance and it's likely that development in dictionary systems will be a crucial selling point for relational databases in the future. Anyone who doubts this should remember the fuss caused when DB2 was released without such integrated facilities.

It should also be remembered that provision of a dictionary, both in table format, and accessible to the same high-level language that is used to access data, is in fact a requirement stated within E Codd's 12 relational database rules. This short chapter examines some aspects of dictionary history and future.

The Information Providers

The concept of the data dictionary has evolved slowly over the years and has risen to eminence largely on the back of the relational database boom. From being simple repositories of file definitions, they are developing not only as central and integrated part of an RDBMS, essential both for internal and external management, but are gradually taking on important roles in the world of system development. In recognition of this more visible and important role, the term 'Data Dictionary' is not really appropriate and ANSI has now coined the term 'Information Resource Dictionary System' (IRDS) for such facilities.

However IRDSs are not as yet in widespread existence and although you can be sure that they will be soon enough, it's more relevant to concentrate on facilities that exist today in this category, and how they originated.

'Dictionary' can be defined as a 'book that lists, usually in alphabetical order, and explains the words of a language' and so it's easy to see why the term has been borrowed by the computer industry and used in the context we so often see today. It's not a new term, and in its simplest and oldest form, computer-based 'data dictionaries' were used to hold file definitions centrally, with the aim of providing a central administration, removing possible replication errors and assisting productivity. There are many examples of such systems in existence today, although they are becoming more and more sophisticated and integrated as time goes by, perhaps a good example is the CDD product found on most VMS-based VAX machines.

With the rise in popularity of the DBMS, or more appropriately the relational variety, such dictionary concepts were quickly integrated into the actual DBMS structure itself. This meant that not only did the system support tables, views and indexes for example, but it also supported a dictionary that defined such physical structures. Dictionaries quickly expanded their role to include details of access permissions, users, resource usage and all sorts of other items of information, which were both logged to the dictionary for reporting purposes, or actually stored there for the RDBMS to use itself in its own management functions.

In fact the dictionary in the relational world is now deemed so important that its existence, and standards defining its structure and accessibility, have been made mandatory for any DBMS to call itself truly relational, and because its presence is now a 'fact of life' even more uses are being added to them every day.

Certainly with the advent of the Fourth Generation Languages, dictionaries are commonly carrying applications code, screen definitions and report formats. A fine example of this can be found in the way the Ingres product has a whole set of dictionary extensions, to hold such definitions created by its Applications By Forms tool set.

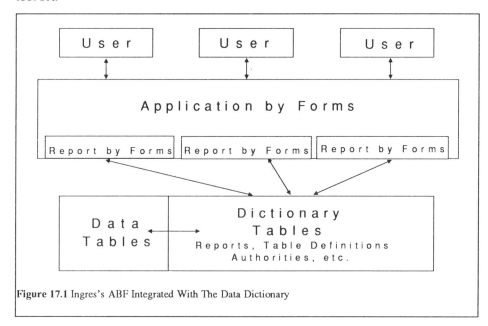

Figure 17.1 Ingres's ABF Integrated With The Data Dictionary

It is particularly in this guise that the term 'data dictionary' is quickly becoming redundant because the dictionary is, in these cases, clearly holding information on a greater range of objects than previously was the case. Looking at this particular example, the various tools that Ingres supplies with its product not only access the dictionary to check on existing objects, but can also be used to create them and even store program, report and screen definitions centrally within the dictionary. Into the future, this will become even more visible as integrated RDBMSs and dictionaries are used, not only in support of the actual building and production work of systems, but also in their design. It's already possible to buy products that will support analysis and design activity, and record both logical and physical database definitions as they are being formulated.

Dictionary History

In order to describe the contents of the older RDBMS dictionaries, it's worth taking a peek into the non-DBMS world. Generally in such an environment, it was possible to find out about existing data structures because not only were their definitions hard coded into applications, which could be examined at any time, but you could also 'see' the individual files on the computer by listing them with operating system commands. However because SQL is interactive, it is quite possible in an RDBMS, to create or alter a table with no hard copy evidence to record the changes made. Because it is then not possible to use operating system facilities to examine such tables, we could find ourselves in some degree of confusion if we did something as simple as forgetting a table name.

The solution of course is to build some system tables in the database itself which would record any such changes as they were made, in a format that the user could access using SQL. Thus the data dictionary was provided to record such information as table, view, index and column definitions on all objects currently within the database, so that the user could list all the tables he had access to, with their column names and definitions. Such dictionaries took on the description of 'active' because not only were they kept up to date at all times by the RDBMS, but the RDBMS itself used them for certain internal management functions. If, for example, an RDBMS cannot manage two tables with the same name, then in order to enforce integrity, the system is likely to hold a list of all table names currently allocated, in order that it might check any CREATE TABLE statement being executed for a duplicate name. In a non-DBMS environment this would be an operating system responsibility and so any such list would be redundant.

The origin of the term 'data dictionary' should therefore be easy to understand because originally these facilities did just that – described the data structures within the database as they were currently defined. However when an SQL statement is executed, the RDBMS must do other things apart from checking for duplicate names in a CREATE TABLE statement. Any statement accessing data will cause checking on all the object names mentioned (typically table and column names), figuring out the availability of any structures, such as indexes, that might be used when accessing the required data, and of course checking whether the particular user involved has the required authority to execute the command on that particular data.

All this type of validation required that the dictionary be expanded to hold such things as access permissions, and user lists, so we can see that from simple beginnings, the dictionary is expanding its role all the time: some varieties hold considerable detail about auditing, journalling, backup and recovery and performance.

The Key Elements

Because the dictionary products supplied by the different vendors vary hugely in quality and content, I prefer not to go into specific detail in this section, but it is possible to state what can be construed as the key elements of a comprehensive dictionary, and it may be of some use to list these here. The key to a dictionary should be its ability to hold:

❏ Detail about all data structures and types of data

❏ Detail about all aspects of the computer systems accessing the database, including programs and external files

❏ Documentary and technical information regarding systems and design features, for example

❏ Detail of the logical structures that are mapped into the database

❏ Detail of relationships between data items and support of domains

❏ Detail of all users, privileges and access rights

❏ Performance and resource usage details.

While we're on the subject of requirements, we should also wish that the dictionary facility be built from relational tables structured using normalising techniques. This requirement should allow for reasonable user access through SQL, and we should not forget that our dictionary should be very well integrated with any 4GLs that access the database. It should also be supplied with tools that can be used to manage the database directly through the dictionary, and here I don't just mean the provision of SQL or a 4GL, but rather a user-friendly sub-system with which a DBA can fully manage all aspects of the database.

The above is a fairly tough list of requirements, and I know of no major RDBMS product that supports a dictionary of this nature. Current systems invariably fall short in the provision of any analysis tools whatsoever, a factor that has in the past led to the provision of separate dictionary type systems being marketed for the more popular products. Examples of such products include the SQL Design Dictionary (SDD) so popular with Oracle users. This represents a successful effort to assist in project development, and adds considerable value to the base products dictionary system.

A very common area where current products fall short, is in the design of the dictionaries themselves and the lack of supplied tools to examine them. These are both factors that are hard to comprehend. It is strange that the structures held in dictionaries are usually so denormalised that any intuitive access is difficult, but the reason behind this is that the system really needs very quick access indeed to dictionary structures, because of the frequency with which they are accessed, and so optimisation, and thus denormalisation, is a requirement.

It should however be quite possible to hide this complexity with a set of system supplied views to help DBA-type management.

There is of course a significant difference between a dictionary that is designed simply to record a certain 'state of play', and one that is to be used in actively assisting in systems analysis and development. At present the former type is the one that you will commonly come across in most commercially available RDBMSs and the latter, as the aforementioned IRDS. Qualifications for this latter group may require the storage (with on-line maintenance access) of descriptive data in the following categories:

❏ Physical data – descriptions of database, files, reports and screen definitions for example

❏ Physical Processes – specifications of processes, macros, compiled transactions, subroutines and job control language

❏ Enterprise level data – typically in the form of Entity Relationship Attribute models these describe the business model which the physical systems support

❏ Enterprise level processes – such as function hierarchies, data flow diagrams and entity life histories. Such items show logically how the business works.

These categories of information are combined by relationships that must also be recorded in the IRDS and without which, the above descriptions become largely meaningless. Such relationships would include those defining:

❏ Which (or how) enterprise processes have been implemented as computer-based processes

❏ How the logical data is mapped in physical tables

❏ Which enterprise processes access which entities

❏ Which computer-base processes access which tables.

The recording of this type of data automatically takes the data dictionary into a whole different world and level of use, but this type of functionality can easily be combined with more traditional types of dictionary function. Such advanced dictionaries, or IRDS, should provide all the facilities to underpin systems analysis, development, implementation, maintenance and production and will I feel, even more so than 4GLs, be responsible for huge applications productivity advances in the future.

Summary

1) One of the 12 relational database rules is that an RDBMS must support a data dictionary defined in terms of relations, and accessed by the same high-level, set oriented language as accesses the rest of the database.

2) From rudimentary beginnings, many dictionaries are becoming increasingly integrated with the actual functioning of the RDBMS they support, and evolving into essential DBA management tools.

3) Data dictionaries should be extendible to form the basis of repositories of application systems-based information, including not only the physical, but also the logical.

4) Integrated dictionaries must look to expand their role into one of full support for applications analysis, design, development, installation, production and maintenance. In short they must support the full development cycle from the birth of a system to its death.

18

The Distributed Relational Database

Just as we're coming to terms with the relational database and begin-
ning to understand its worth, we're now being forced into the even more
demanding world of the distributed database. There are two questions
begging for answers:

❏ What is a distributed relational database?

❏ Are we ready for it?

The answer to the first question is easily explained, and I think it fair to say,
in answer to the second, that the same people are ready now for the
distributed product as accepted the base product eight years ago. It's
still early days, and as people move toward developing corporate data
strategies, the need for distributing knowledge (not necessarily data) will
become paramount.

The Radical Approach

It would be negligent in a book of this nature, to ignore the distributed database
facilities within the leading relational products. Although at the present time there are
very few installations implementing them or benefiting from them, there is little
doubt, that just as the dawn of relational databases was greeted with a great deal of
confusion followed by an almost hysterical acceptance, we are currently in the
confused state prior to the acceptance of the distributed product. When its scope is
more fully defined, implemented and understood, its significance will be more fully
appreciated. Thankfully, this is likely to take some time, simply because of the sheer
scale of investment and foresight required to take the move toward this somewhat
radical (at least for now) approach.

Before moving ahead it would seem wise to take the opportunity to clarify the
concept of distribution in two areas.

Distributed Processing

This technique, in a variety of different guises, has been utilised for several years and in its simplest form has allowed people to dial up computers from remote terminals over telephone lines for some quarter of a century. Its context here refers however, to an architecture in which a database resides on a different machine to the user process accessing it. To put this in a different way, the front- and back-end processes are on different machines. Such a mechanism will obviously necessitate some form of communication capability between the machine and depends entirely on a complete logical and physical separation between the front- and back-end processes and processing. We can illustrate distributed processing with the diagram in Figure 18.1.

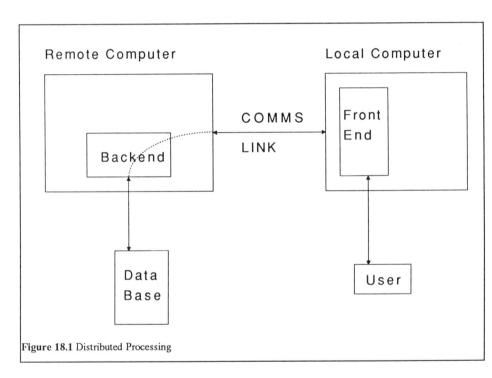

Figure 18.1 Distributed Processing

Such distribution, as this example portrays, is fairly widespread, and is the function of the Ingres Net product to name just one. With this utility, a user can run an interactive SQL (ISQL) session on a VAX machine which accesses transparently, an Ingres database on another VAX. Typically these VAXes will be connected by an Ethernet Local Area Network (LAN), but the detail of this connectivity, and in fact the detail of the separation of data from processing, should be entirely transparent to the user. This transparency is certainly not achieved in some of today's distributed processing networks, but is a goal towards which all should aim.

Distributed Database

This concept is fundamentally different from distributed processing, and is considerably more complex to attain. So much so, that at the time of writing, is not in existence, a product that will support this architecture, in all the areas I will discuss later, is not in existence. A distributed database environment assumes that processing must to some extent be distributed also, but the fundamental principle is that the data available to a single user resides on more than one machine. Of utmost importance to the concept is again, the requirement that the user need not concern himself in any way with where that data is in fact stored.

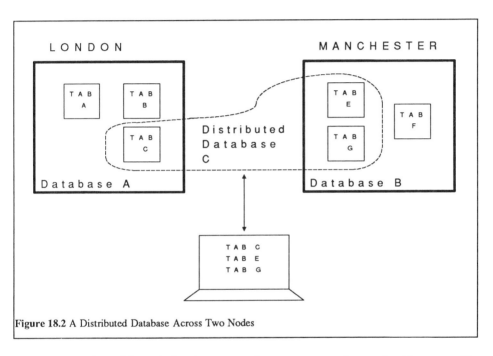

Figure 18.2 A Distributed Database Across Two Nodes

To recap on these ideas, let's picture a salesman out on the road with a portable computer to give him access to some corporate data held elsewhere. This is in itself a valid case of distributed processing, as the salesman connects his PC to the PSTN and logs onto a remote host to execute his query and retrieve required results. If he has some application software on his PC – a prompt-driven query screen for example, into which he types his requirements, and this software itself handles all aspects of the communications, then this is simply a case of more complex distributed processing. The ball game changes however, if the communications between PC and host connect the salesman to a network hosting a distributed database.

Although the salesman must still logon to one machine, the principle is that his query may be accessing data held in a database on this host, or any other host participating in the distributed database, and that the mechanisms behind the retrieval of the desired result set are completely transparent to the salesman. This is powerful stuff indeed.

In this chapter I wish to focus mainly on the distributed database and the facilities that such products should be aiming to provide. Already in existence and published, are guidelines defining such facilities, but as I have already stressed there are currently no products that provide all of them. Having said this, several vendors are marketing products that provide a subset of these facilities, and so the potential user should not be put off from closer inspection – they should remember that few base relational database products implement all the major rules of the relational model, and some in fact have deliberately chosen not to do so for some very good reasons.

Perhaps the first two products to have found favour in the market-place are the Ingres Star implementation from Ingres and SQL*Star from Oracle, and these will undoubtedly be the forerunners of many other flavours. Perhaps the most eagerly awaited distributed product (in the real sense), is DB2 which will in effect give the seal of approval to the technology. This product, already partially available, will bring to fruition years of research and development on the IBM R* project – the original distributed version of the relational database System R. Indeed it is no coincidence that the distributed database has followed the progress of the relational database because it is only relational technology that makes such systems feasible in the first place. For a database to be distributed it must be relational because older style architectures are simply not adequate, for reasons that should become apparent later in this chapter.

Firstly therefore, let's identify what constitutes a distributed database system, before proceeding with a description of the criteria to which such systems should conform.

In essence a distributed database system is a collection of sites or nodes connected by communication lines whereby:

1) Each participating node houses a relational database

2) These databases are themselves fully functional within their own location

3) A logical (or virtual if preferred) global distributed database is defined incorporating elements of each of the participating databases in order to emulate a single occurrence of a database.

It seems almost rude in a book like this to refer to communications, but of course every true distributed system will be built on top of some networking system. Ingres Star, for example is built on top of Ingres/Net, and such software systems will in turn be built on some commercially available architecture such as SNA, or DECNET. Ingres/Net currently runs predominantly on TCP/IP and DECNET.

It is not entirely fair at this stage, to dismiss the more technical communications issues. A distributed system depends heavily on its mode of communications both for its everyday function and its ability to connect to different hardware and different networks. The preferred products should conform to the Open Systems Interconnect (OSI) model, and its pleasing to note a high degree of commitment in this area by the majority of RDBMS vendors.

The OSI argument is now accepted by most, and the aim of its network model is to provide layered interfacing between differing levels of processing. Each layer is responsible for one type of communications function, passing information to higher or lower layers lying between the user and the physical communications link. For those interested in the OSI model, Ingres implements it on an Ethernet connection as below.

	Layer	Product
7	Presentation	ABF, QBF etc
6	Application	Ingres/Net
5	Session	Ingres/Net
4	Transport	Decnet, SNA, TCP/IP etc
3	Network	Ethernet
2	Datalink	HDLC, SDLC etc
1	Physical	COAX, RS232 etc

Figure 18.3 The ISO Communications Model with reference to Ingres

Perhaps it's more clearly shown with a diagram:

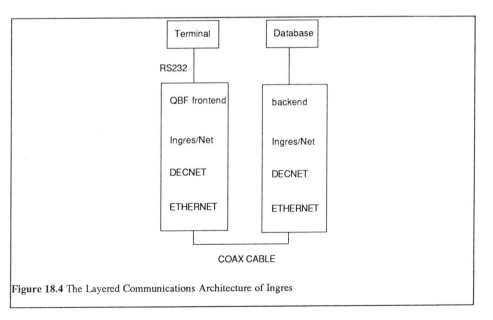

Figure 18.4 The Layered Communications Architecture of Ingres

Communications aside, the fundamentals of a distributed architecture as described above, are fairly straightforward, even though it must be pointed out that the separation of nodes need not be physical in a sense that two databases linked in a distributed fashion could reside on the same machine. Such a scenario might be used to aid migration between development, testing and production systems or, in the world of Ingres, to allow an application access to both an existing Ingres database and a set of VAX RMS files through a Gateway product. (I shall discuss Gateways later).

Having therefore covered some of the more physical aspects, it's time to discuss the makings of a fully distributed database. Just as there is a set of rules to which relational databases should conform, there is a set that defines the scope of the distributed version, and a good place to start is to describe what has been defined as the level 0 rule, indicating its dominance over all others.

Rule 0, and I've already hinted at its content, states that a user of a distributed system should under all circumstances see it exactly as he would expect to see a non-distributed system.

This of course means that the software, DBA and perhaps Systems Programming teams, need to do some work behind the scenes, to preserve the physical implementation from all the users involved. This leads to the first real rule which states that all of the local sites defined as comprising a distributed database should be able to participate autonomously when required, in standard database activity. All data items within the distributed database should in fact belong to a single site, and such matters of security and integrity of that subset of the total data should be managed at a local level. In essence this means that the distributed database consists of several other databases (in whole or part), and that each of these participating databases must be able to function independently and in its own right.

Taking this idea further, it is also of importance that an application, which ran successfully on a database prior to its incorporation in a distributed version, should continue to do so unchanged and with no performance penalties, if its database is later incorporated into such a distributed system. Unfortunately, it must be said that the detail of such total site autonomy, is not currently proving possible to achieve because the requirement, of having no site dependent on any other, is contrary to the current methods of implementing distributed strategies, as we will see later. However, if it is possible to achieve local autonomy to any reasonable extent, so that an entire system need never depend on a single central site, we will have achieved a highly desirable state of affairs in reducing both potential bottlenecks and vulnerability. However in stating the case for autonomy, we must not forget that to achieve distributed data, many previously centralised database management functions must themselves be distributed, and in this list we need to include dictionary management, locking, optimisation and recovery, all subjects which will be discussed later.

I have already stressed the need for the users to be unaware of participation in a distributed system, and this concept is termed that of *location independence* or *location transparency*. Again whilst easy to state requirements, the complexity of attaining this goal is enormous, so let's take some time to see how the distributed database may exist and the problems associated with it.

If we imagine several separate databases, located at different nodes in a network of some description, a common way for them to be defined within the scope of a distributed database is through the definition of a virtual database.

Thus in the example below D1, D2 and D3 are physical and independent databases at sites S1, S2 and S3 respectively, and V1 is a distributed database consisting of tables from each database. The dictionary for V1 sits at a further site S4, where logical entries point to the real tables and describe both their location and a synonym by which these tables may be known to all V1 users. V1 can be accessed by users at S4 just as if it is a local database, and the DBA of V1 can make it accessible to any other sites, by entering pointers to the V1 dictionary in the database dictionaries located there.

The virtual database, defined at a single node, will have its own dictionary, but the content of this dictionary will be pointers as it were, to real tables existing in other real databases. Just as the relational databases can support views defined across many tables, so the distributed relational database can be thought of as a view across multiple databases. Just as views can have different names from their underlying tables, so virtual tables can have different names from their physical counterparts.

Up to this point, I have ignored most of the detail involved in implementing such strategies. However I have mentioned, there is a need to distribute certain key functions of the DBMS, and three of these are certainly query optimisation, transaction management and locking. By considering these in some detail, an idea of the complexity of this model should become apparent.

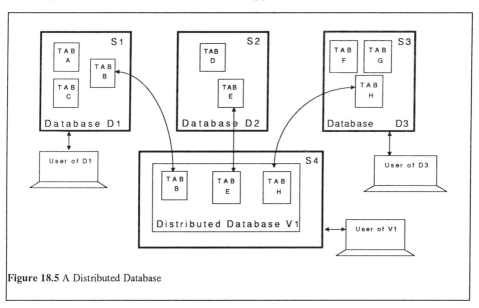

Figure 18.5 A Distributed Database

Distributed Optimisation

Because SQL is written at such a high level, there are many ways – often termed plans – in which an SQL statement can be executed, and thus the optimiser, as I have previously called it, whilst important in any relational database, is of absolute criticality when data and processing are distributed. In previous types of database, performance was largely dependent on the quality of the applications programmer, and if the programmer chose a poor programming strategy, there is no way that the system could convert it to a good one. This is much less the case in a world of SQL and RDBMSs where the incorporation of a query optimiser should ensure that the cheapest (or quickest) method of executing queries will be used no matter how the SQL is formulated. In the distributed world, the best QEP will be evolved with respect to all sorts of resource usage at the many different sites involved, and any cost of communication between them. This last factor in reality may prove to be the largest consideration (and cost factor).

Let's put together a simple example, based on our previous illustration, to highlight the importance of optimisation, especially within the light of potential communications costs.

Suppose someone enters an SQL statement at S3 which performs an equi-join on a table at S1 (1,000 rows) with a table at S2 (1,000,000 rows). Global optimisation at S3 should determine the source of the data, and that some type of data transfer and sort/merge operation will be required, but should it move the table at S1 to S2, the table at S2 to S1 or perhaps both tables to S3 to perform the join? It is fairly clear that the most efficient and low-cost operation, with respect to communications costs, is to move the table at S1 to S2, but the consequence of making a mistake could be very expensive indeed. Once the data has been moved to S2, the local optimiser should work out the best plan to most efficiently execute the statement (which has of course been transmitted from S3 to S2 in the meanwhile), and deliver the result set back to S3. To put it bluntly, there is a lot going on, and many points of potential failure, and this was only a simply query on data at two sites.

Distributed Transaction Management

In terms of transaction management there are two major fundamentals to juggle with, namely recovery and concurrency. Both of these have already been dealt with in the scope of the single database but require extended consideration in the distributed environment. A 'distributed' transaction may require, in order to complete, the execution of code at many sites, and it is usual to have a 'coordinator' process to take overall charge of the query execution and 'agent' processes on each participating node to action the distributed parts of it. Now, all these agents must be controlled so that their work is performed in parallel, in as much as that if one agent commits its part of the transaction successfully, then so must they all. Conversely, if just one agent fails, all agents must perform a rollback of all activity in that transaction being carried out by that agent. The need for a coordinator however, which is usually, but not necessarily, at the site of the instigation of the transaction, enables this type of activity to be possible but also, unfortunately, ensures a transgression of the 'local autonomy' rule. This is true because the very nature of the coordinator/agent relationship, which is governed by a protocol called the Two Phase Commit, ensures a master/slave dependency in which the agent must obey the instruction of the coordinator to either commit or rollback. The problems with transaction management in a distributed environment have proved, and are still proving, to be of some magnitude, and it is probably true to say that it is the major reason why this architecture is so rarely implemented in its entirety at present.

Distributed Locking

Although there are several ways of providing concurrency control, a system of object locking predominates in the database environment, and works in fundamentally the same way in distributed and non-distributed systems. The implementation of locking in the distributed system has proved difficult to implement, and there have been major problems with both Ingres and Oracle with regard to the locking of objects across nodes in a VAX cluster, for example.

In general local sites should provide local locking, but some scheme of global lock management is a necessity because it is quite possible to achieve deadlock between different sites in the same manner as between different tables in a single database. Unfortunately in a global distributed deadlock, no single site has enough information to detect the deadlock without resorting to some continual communication with other nodes, and this communication can add extra overheads on already loaded lines. A scheme of simply timing-out in deadlock situations is favoured by most systems, and whilst simple to implement, it can be inefficient because transactions may be timed out unnecessarily. Invariably, much application code is required to handle the deadlock/time-out in a user-friendly manner.

Helping The Communications Overhead

There seems to be no getting away from the communications overheads implicit in the distributed system, but there are some helpful features which should be supported by the RDBMS. I hinted that a distributed system must in essence be relational, and some of the reason why this is so is found in the need for data fragmentation and replication to minimise communications and maximise availability.

As an example, if we had a customer file being accessed from New York and London, but held entirely in New York, we would expect to be a fairly large customer of one of the information carrier services, while we continually shift data across the Atlantic, and it is this type of problem that needs some sort of assistance from our RDBMS. Fragmentation is a technique that allows the logical and physical division of our Customer table into the databases at our two sites, so that all New

York customer details are held locally at New York and all London records are held in London. Such a scheme is termed horizontal fragmentation and is easily achieved by key field values. The whole table is therefore simply a union of these fragments.

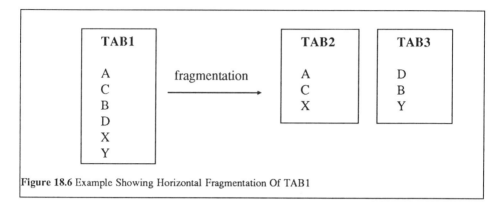

Figure 18.6 Example Showing Horizontal Fragmentation Of TAB1

It is also possible to vertically partition a table simply by holding different columns in different places, and in such an example the complete table is a join of its constituent fragments. The case for this type of fragmentation is not so simple to justify, and if implemented, would usually need to be 'non-loss' in terms that the primary key column would need to be present in each and every fragment.

TAB1				TAB2		TAB3	
COL1	COL2	COL3		COL1	COL2	COL1	COL2
A	1	2		A	1	A	2
B	5	7	fragmentation	B	5	B	7
T	3	9		T	3	T	9

Figure 18.7 Virtual Fragmentation of TAB1 Into Two Parts

The two types of fragmentation must share an important common characteristic however, and that is one based on a very common distributed theme. The user of a fragmented table, no matter of what type, must be unaware that it is anything other than a normal relation. Just as we require location transparency, we also require fragmentation transparency and this is indeed critical to the user and application.

Not a world away from fragmentation is the concept of data replication, and this must be implemented again in both a global and transparent manner. For the sake of both efficiency and availability, our distributed relational database may need to facilitate the holding of more than one copy of a table or fragment at different nodes in the database. Such replication should achieve increased performance as applications may be able to operate on local copies of data, instead of having to communicate with remote sites. Resilience should also improve, as activity should be able to continue as long as there is just one copy of a fragment of data available within the whole database.

Replication of read-only data is not a serious weakness, but problems are apparent when entering update mode, there will be more than one copy of each record to be updated, and each will, by definition, be at a different site. There are many conceptual ways of overcoming this difficulty, and perhaps the most common one relies on defining one occurrence of the data as being the prime copy. The advantage here is that it is deemed necessary only to update the prime copy in 'real time' – the other copies being updated at a more convenient point later.

Of course it is not difficult to spot the weaknesses in this argument, as it neatly breaks many of the major principles of the distributed model, and in fact the database concept itself.

Just as a key factor up to now has been 'transparency', so must replication be seamless to the user, in that he must not be able to address specific occurrences of replicated data. Obviously this is a problem, because only one occurrence is necessarily up-to-date and in answer to this problem the concept of the 'snap shot' is coming into favour.

Similar in syntax to the view, a snapshot is a data definition and query that is executed at predefined times of the day, with the result set being retained as a temporary user-addressable table of data. Snapshot data can be replicated and users will know whether they are querying current or snapshot data and make their choices accordingly.

There are therefore a multitude of technical and organisational problems to be overcome in order to implement a true, fully functioning distributed database, and there are many levels of complexity that I have not yet touched on. Imagine for example the difficulty in implementing full referential integrity checking across a distributed database. Many of the problems do cease of course, if we are not concerned with update, delete and insert activity so let us proceed to outline two fundamental types of distributed systems.

Homogeneous and Heterogeneous Systems

There are two types of distributed database namely the homogeneous variety, in which all the participating databases are all of the same type (all Sybase RDBMSs for example), and the more purposeful and realistic, heterogeneous system which is a distributed database combining many different types of database.

In this chapter up to now, I have been implicitly referring to the homogeneous variety but the latter type, which is much more likely to represent real world requirements, will obviously be a little more complicated to achieve. Whilst it has not proved too difficult, or too non-profitable, to achieve hardware and operating system transparency across more common computers, there is real value and difficulty in achieving transparency between different types of relational database which are to work in cooperation. The mechanisms that are allowing this type of communication bring us nicely onto the subject of gateways.

As pointed out above, the real world will most likely require a distributed database to be comprised of databases supplied by different vendors, and it is apparent that the ability to talk to, or participate with DB2, in a distributed database is becoming of prime concern to the independent vendors.

The way that this communication is being designed is as a series of software interfaces loosely called gateways, and the occurrence of specific gateway software, or the ease of providing it, is proving to be of commercial advantage in the vendor community.

So, what is a gateway? To illustrate the answer let's imagine an Oracle distributed database which requires the inclusion of data held in an Ingres database. In such a situation, the onus is on Oracle to implement a software interface that will allow Oracle SQL commands to be interpreted by the Ingres system, and Ingres data to be readable by Oracle. It is this software interface that would be termed the gateway.

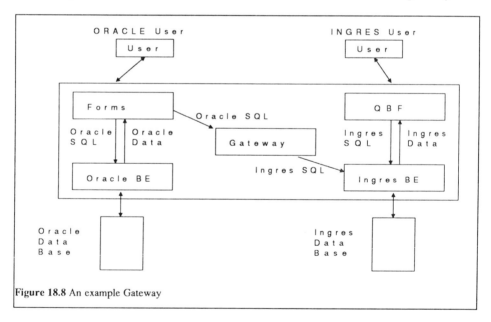

Figure 18.8 An example Gateway

Of course we start from the advantageous situation of nominating two products that both use SQL, but you will realise after reading various parts of this text, that the two dialects of SQL are far from similar. There are many technical issues to be addressed when one product is expected to communicate with one from a different vendor, and these include:

1) Enabling the target database environment to understand the SQL being sent from the source database.

2) Enabling the source database to be able to understand, and if necessary repackage, data coming back from the target (data values, messages, return codes etc).

3) Mapping the target dictionary to the source dictionary so that queries formulated at the source can be validated and actioned correctly on the target.

4) Conversion between the two systems' data types and formats – a subset of the above problem.

5) Coordination in the aforementioned 'two-phase commit' protocol if update activity is to be allowed and, if it is, then the added complication of coordinating transaction management.

6) Maintaining a consistent locking strategy across databases which actually lock resources in quite different ways.

7) Making full use of each product's optimisation strategies.

The list can be extended further, but the above subset should serve as a warning that the matter is not trivial. One should also bear in mind that a single gateway only provides a master/slave type access between the two specific databases and that communication is one way. To have the two products participate equally in the global database would likely require two gateways.

Before moving off the subject, we should consider the non-relational database and its participation in a distributed system. It is quite possible, and in fact common, to provide gateways to non-relational databases and those such as IMS, IDMS, dBASE and even the RMS files of VAX/VMS are available to play their part in combination with certain other products.

It's true that the data held in these databases will often be in a format that makes it difficult, if not impossible, to map to a relational type dictionary, or in fact, relational type tables, and so reality dictates that these interfaces will be limited, and for a long time probably read-only. Their benefit in the short term, include that of providing possible upgrade paths of systems from perhaps 3 to 4GL and this can be a factor of considerable importance.

A Different Approach

Whilst I have not deliberately set out to discourage interest in the distributed product, it would be dangerous to imagine that it is a fully-functional, reliable and useful product at present. There is another approach which becomes increasingly potent if we are concerned with very large quantities of data and/or achieving fast response time.

The original concept of the database was that of the provision of a single, centralised pool or sump, of corporate data. This concept heralded many advantages, two of these which are of considerable importance are, that control of data could be centralised, and that data should not be replicated. With the coming of the distributed database, which is partly a necessity because of weak technical advancement and poor data strategies, both of these advantages could be quite effectively lost overnight. So is there an alternative?

Technology at this present time says 'yes there is' and it comes in the form of large, very fast database machines of which the previously mentioned Teradata DBC/1012 is the world leader. Imagine a machine that can:

❑ Hold effectively, unlimited amounts of data in relational format accessed purely by SQL

❑ Has all the facilities expected of an RDBMS

❑ Can connect remotely or locally, at high speed with all major computers servicing the commercial world today

❑ Can effectively process thousands of transactions per second

❑ Offers the potential of thousands of MIPS to a single user.

It is these staggering statistics that make me believe that for companies with huge data volumes which require even reasonable response time, the answer for a long time to come may lie, once again, in centralising data and distributing the processing requirements to the areas that would otherwise form nodes in a distributed database environment. It may not be as esoterically pleasing as the distributed relational database but it is technology that is available today.

Summary

1) The concept of distributed processing and the distributed database are very different, although the latter does presume and rely on, the existence of the former.

2) Full implementation of the distributed database is proving to be very problematical. There are huge difficulties, in both the management of data, and management of the fundamental functions that become constituents of the RDBMS when moving into distributed mode.

3) For some time into the future, implementation of fully functional distributed RDBMSs is likely to be very demanding and expensive, for vendor and user alike.

4) In many ways, the distributed database, or the practicalities required to make them work, will be in contravention of some fundamental database concepts.

5) Before embarking on distributed strategies, the real alternative of centralised data with distributed processing should be revisited in the light of advancing technology.

References

Proceedings of the Sixth British Conference on Databases (BNCOD 6), Cambridge 1988

Information Processing Systems – Distributed Transaction Processing OSI Document ISO/TC/97/SL21

S. Ceri and G. Pelagatti, Distributed Databases, Principles and Systems *McGraw-Hill*, New York, 1984

Glossary

Access Control	a major function of a DBMS lies in controlling the use of the same items of data by many users. Access control facilities are those used by the DBMS in determining which users can perform what operations on the data under its control. In relational databases these facilities are provided primarily through a subset of SQL commands.
ACCESSDB	a program provided with Ingres to assign various privileges to the user community.
ADD	a data dictionary tool that can be used with Ingres.
After Image File	a mechanism used by the Oracle RDBMS to record changes being made to data as they occur. Such a record can be used to recover a database after major failure and data loss.
ANSI	American National Standards Institute.
Asynchronous Readahead	a mechanism used by Oracle to pre-fetch blocks of data to optimise full table scan activity.
Attribute	an item of data that describes an entity.
Audit	a general term used in the database world, to indicate some type of usage or access monitoring.
Back End	for those systems using a client/server architecture, the 'back end' is the process in direct communication with the data and organises all access to it.
Backup	the taking of a copy of data to provide security against loss or corruption of the original.
Before Image File	a mechanism used by Oracle, up to version 5, to ensure transaction integrity by holding copies of data that is currently being changed in its unchanged form during the life time of a transaction.
Before Image Writer	the Oracle process that writes data to the Before Image File, prior to it being updated in the database itself.

Bit -Mapped Index	a mechanism of indexing which allows the combination of many indexes on different columns in the same table. The technique is useful to optimise access when each individual index is only weakly selective.
Block	takes different meanings, depending on which DBMS or operating system is the target, but a block in general is a unit of data storage, either logical or physical.
Btree	a common method of indexing into database structures where there is an index entry for every data row.
Buffer Writer	the Oracle process responsible for read and write activity on the database tables.
Cartesian Product	a method of joining tables, where the result table comprises a set in which every row in every table is matched with every row in every other table.
Cluster	either a term used to define logically associated AMPs in a Teradata DBC/1012 machine, or a method used to organise data rows in a relational database.
COBOL	Common Business Oriented Language – the most commonly used procedural programming language today.
Column Constraints	a relational integrity facility allowing certain rules to be defined on a column that concern the quality of the data that can be held in that column.
COMMIT	the mechanism of telling the DBMS that your current transaction is finished, and you wish the data to be written to the database.
Compiled Transaction	a mechanism of holding pre-canned SQL transactions in compiled form, in the database, for immediate execution by privileged users
Compression	a space saving mechanism used on indexes and data rows. Typically repeating characters or strings are removed.
Correlated queries	an SQL term to describe the situation where a subquery is evaluated once for every row selected by the main query.
Data Dictionary	a utility holding data which describes in various levels of detail, the application databases for which they exist.

DECNET	DEC's proprietary networking system.
DDL	Data Definition Language – a subset of SQL commands used to build, alter and destroy database objects.
DEADLOCK	a situation where transactions cannot complete because they are each waiting for an object that one of the other transactions owns exclusively.
Deferred Write	a mechanism of reducing I/O to a database by utilising memory more effectively.
Dense Index	an index such as a Btree which holds entries for every data row.
Detached Process	a collective name for the Oracle processes that manage the database.
Disk Array	a mechanism of spreading the work load over many disk drives. Such architectures can have great effect on both access time and reliability.
Disk Shadowing	a hardware solution to data security which relies on always having an identical copy of a disk in the operational configuration. If one disk is lost, its shadow takes over immediately.
Distributed Database	when more than one database can be combined into a single virtual database, which the user can use as though he was accessing a single non-distributed database.
Distributed Processing	a scheme where the process serving the user directly, is not the one that is preforming database access on his behalf.
DML	Manipulation Language – a subset of SQL including INSERT, DELETE, SELECT and UPDATE.
Domain Constraints	validation rules that can be centrally defined and actioned, and pertain to domains.
Duplicate Row	a row that is identical to another row in the same relation.
Entity	a data analysis term used to describe a 'thing' or 'object' about which things are known.

ERA	entity, relationship, attribute, – a term used to describe a type of data analysis modelling.
Ethernet	a communications protocol compliant with the seven layer ISO standard.
Explain	a program provided with some RDBMSs that will tell the user how an SQL statement will be performed, and what the expected cost of it will be in terms of machine resources.
Fallback	a method used on the Teradata DBC/1012 of maintaining a copy of every row recorded on a different processor to protect against processor failure.
Fast Commit	a mechanism, favoured by several RDBMS vendors of reducing database I/O to achieve high transaction throughput.
Fault Tolerance	a term used to indicate that a system has some protection against any part of it failing.
Fillfactor	the percentage by which disk blocks are initially filled by either index entries or data rows.
Fragmentation	a mechanism of splitting a table up into various parts of relevance to distributed systems. Typically the parts will be held at different nodes to aid performance.
Functional Dependence	a word used in data analysis to describe a relationship, where the value of an attribute associated with an entity, depends on the value of the primary key of that entity.
Foreign Key	an attribute in a table that is also the primary key in another table. Typically, foreign keys are often used as access paths into the table in which they reside.
Front End	in a client/server architecture, this will be the process that communicates directly with the user.
Gateway	an item of software or hardware that allows the front end program of one type of database to communicate with the back end of another.
Group Commit	a mechanism for reducing the amount of I/O required to support high transaction throughput rates.

Hash	a method of providing fast access into data tables by converting the contents of the primary key into a logical row address.
Hash Synonym	when two different key values are hashed to the same value, they will be physically stored together – they will be hash synonyms.
Heap	the term used to describe the situation when rows in a table are not stored in any order, or have no indexes built upon them.
Heterogeneous	generally used to define distributed databases when the individual systems are not of the same type.
Hierarchical	a structure used to build and manage many traditional databases such as IMS.
Homogeneous	generally used to define distributed databases when the individual systems are of the same type.
IMS	a hierarchical DBMS popular in the IBM world.
IMS/Fastpath	an extension to IMS designed to support high transaction processing levels.
Index	structures built on data tables to provide quicker access to individual rows.
INGRES	the RDBMS supplied by Ingres.
Intersect	a relational operation which selects rows common the more than one table.
Inverted List	a database access method favoured by some notable systems such as ADABAS.
IOR	the Oracle utility for initialising, starting and stopping databases.
ISAM	an indexing method provided as an alternative within the Ingres system.
Join	the fundamental relational operator which allows rows from two or more tables to be combined on common values.
Key	a column or group of columns in a single relation that can be used to uniquely identify a row in that same relation.

Lock	a mechanism of preventing multi-user access to the same object of data, an action that might result in corruption of that data.
Lock Escalation	the process of changing a locking mechanism to be more restrictive.
Metadata	data which describes other data. Such information usually resides in a data dictionary where it helps both the DBMS and the DBA manage the database resource.
MTBF	Mean Time Between Failures is a term used to measure the reliability of various items. The time will be the average period that expires between the same component failing twice.
Nested Join	a fast way of doing a join, which involves selection from one table and direct access into the other.
Normalisation	a data analysis technique used to ensure that data in a model is logically compatible with other data in the same model, and held without unnecessary redundancy.
Null	a term used to describe either that a value has not yet been provided or that it is inapplicable for it to exist.
OLTP	On-Line Transaction Processing – applications that require interactive response from a user, and are usually characterised by requiring fast response time.
Optimisation	the process of determining the most cost effective way of executing a database query.
Optimisedb	an Ingres utility that collects statistics about the data distribution in tables.
ORACLE	a Relational DBMS supplied by Oracle Corp.
Overflow	the condition which arises when a row cannot fit into its designated disk block, and must therefore be placed elsewhere.
Parsing	the operation that analyses SQL and builds operational steps that can be executed on the machine.
Portable	the ability to move software and data from one machine or DBMS to another.
Predicate clause	selection criteria containing no AND, OR or NOT but including operators such as =, !=, IS, IS NOT, <, > etc.

Primary Key	an analysis term for the column or group of columns that uniquely identifies a row.
Product Join	a type of join where qualifying rows from one table are compared with every qualifying row from the other.
Project	a relational operation in which a subset of columns is selected from the total pool of those available.
Query Execution Plan	a series of steps that can be executed to satisfy an SQL transaction.
Query Optimisation	the process of creating and evaluating the cheapest possible query execution plan.
Redundancy	a term that is used to infer duplication, either for the purposes of resilience, or, in analysis, to indicate replicated data.
Recovery	the process of returning data to an acceptable operational state after some type of failure.
Referential Integrity	the requirement for every item of detail to have in existence, a master.
Restrict	a relational operation which selects only a subset of rows from a table.
RMS	a file system supplied by DEC, for its VMS operating system.
Roll Back	the mechanism which removes any data changes made by a transaction, unless that transaction completes in its entirety.
Roll Forward	a mechanism that can apply data changes from a journal to a database that has been corrupted or destroyed.
Scalable Performance	a term used to infer that performance can be incrementally improved and forecast accurately.
SDD	the design dictionary tool from Oracle Corp.
Server Architecture	a database architecture in which access to the database itself is performed as a central service to the user community.
Snapshot	a mechanism by which data is replicated in a RDBMS on a systematic and regular bases to improve accessibility.

Sort/Merge Join	a type of join which relies on both tables being in the same join column order.
Sparse Index	an index such as ISAM in which there need not be an index entry for every row.
SQL	Structured Query Language – the standard language for accessing relational data.
Timeout	an activity that happens after a defined length of time following deadlock detection. One of the offending transactions will be timed out - it will be aborted and rolled back, allowing the others to progress.
Trigger	a facility in which predefined SQL statements will be issued depending on the result of others, or some other user activity.
TP1	a 'standard' transaction that is often used as the basis of database performance measurement.
Transient Journal	the journals that record data prior to its being changed, in order to facilitate transaction roll back.
Transitive Dependence	a term used in data analysis to describe the relationship between a primary key and an attribute, where the value of the attribute depends not only on the primary key, but also on some other attribute associated with the same entity.
Two Phase Commit	the protocol ensuring that in a distributed database, a distributed transaction completes or fails in total.
SYBASE	one of the commercially available relational DBMSs.
Transaction	SQL instructions that must either complete or fail together.
Third Normal Form	a technique for normalising data.
View	a relational construct enabling the creating of dynamic and virtual 'windows' onto real database tables.
Union	a relational operation used to combine the result sets of similar queries.
VSAM	a popular mechanism of organising files in the IBM world.

Index

joins
    product, 132
    sort/merge, 132
    table, 135
journalling, 70, 191, 191

K

key value, 119 - 122
key, foreign, 170
key, primary, 120, 123, 170
keys, compound, 53

L

language,
    assembler, 2
    fifth generation, 4
    first generation, 2
    fourth generation, 4, 23
    third generation database, 4, 23
    procedural, 39
layer,
    conceptual, 21
    external, 21
    internal, 22
    logical, 21, 23, 52, 91
    native, 21 - 23, 32, 34
    physical, 21, 22, 32, 34, 52, 91
layered interfacing, 205
leaf index block, 116
level 1 environments, 12
level 2 environments, 12, 14
level 3 environments, 12, 14
level 4 environments, 13
level 5 environments, 13
level locking, 157
level privilege, 165
local area network, 202
location independence, 206
location transparency, 206
lock escalation, 157, 158
lock management, 209
locking, 70, 100, 119, 131, 140, 149, 206, 207
    distributed, 209
    granularity, 155, 157
    modes, 156
    row level, 149
    strategy, 139, 213
locks, 68
    row, 154
    shared, 154
    table definition, 154
log table, 188
logical
    address, 121
    child pointer, 28
    data independence, 93
    data model, 51
    layer, 21, 23, 52, 91
    level, 21, 55
    model, 27

logical tables, 55
LOGTABLE, 140
look-up, 133
lost update, 144, 150

M

machine resource usage, 188
mail boxes, 65
management information systems (MIS), 13, 14, 73, 85, 101, 191
many-to-many relationship, 32
MASTERTABLE, 140
metadata, 19, 88
modelling, entity relationship, 5
modify, 121, 121
MODIFY, 99, 114
multi-processor hardware, 80
multi-server architectures, 80
multi-server database architecture, 79
multi-user database systems, 146
multi-user environment, 144
multi-volume tables, 81
multiple server architecture, 63

N

native layer, 21 - 23, 32, 34
NCR Corp, 146
nested joins, 133, 133
network, 91
    architecture, 34
    database, 36
    sets, 35
node, 79
nodes, 206, 207, 209, 214
Non Stop SQL, 76
non-distributed database, 93
non-loss join, 91, 92
non-unique indexes, 123, 130
normalisation, 222
NOT NULL, 107
null values, 89, 102, 107, 171, 173
NULL, 89, 130, 175

O

OLTP (on-line transaction processing), 74 - 77, 81 - 85, 146, 158, 187, 194
one-to-many relationship, 173
Open Systems Interconnect (OSI), 205
operating system access control, 162
optimisation, 206, 207
optimisation strategy, 213
optimisation, global, 208
optimiser, 127, 128, 130 - 133, 137, 208
Oracle, 7, 8, 62, 65 - 72, 76, 82, 87, 99, 102 - 107, 114, 118, 121, 130, 134, 135, 142, 143, 153, 157, 163, 164, 165, 184 - 186, 191, 194, 198, 204
Oracle forms, 155
Oracle query optimiser, 71
Oracle, warm starting, 65